Y0-BXX-184

San Francisco
Medical Center
LIBRARY

A DOCTOR'S REPORT ON DIANETICS

A DOCTOR'S REPORT ON

DIANETICS

Theory and Therapy

---

by J . A . WINTER, M.D.

Introduction by

FREDERICK PERLS, M.D., Ph.D.

JULIAN PRESS, INC. · NEW YORK

PUBLISHED BY JULIAN PRESS, INC.

8 WEST 40TH STREET, NEW YORK 18

PUBLISHED SIMULTANEOUSLY IN CANADA

BY THE COPP CLARK COMPANY, LTD.

COPYRIGHT 1951 BY JOSEPH A. WINTER, M.D.

PRINTED IN THE UNITED STATES OF AMERICA

BOOK DESIGN BY EDGARD CIRLIN

RC461
W78d
1951
Davies Pd

TO MY WIFE

84101

CONTENTS

—— INTRODUCTION ——

At THE TIME when psychoanalysis itself was commonly dismissed as a "crackpot" theory, I learned not to be intimidated by name calling. As one who has attempted to make contributions to psychoanalytic theory, I realize now, as I realized then, that the science of psychotherapy is not a closed or finished one. The division of psychotherapists into mutually hostile "schools" has been more destructive to the young science of psychotherapy than the earlier hostility of the layman; each school in its battle against the other has acted as if it had all the answers and, for the most part, has ignored insights of a rival school. Name-calling has become a substitute for independent thinking, the lifeblood of any science. The interests of this science (as well as of those who come to its practitioners for help) demand that I remain sensitive to the ideas of others. Insights, even though badly or inadequately formulated, are worth investigating. The history of science is full of examples of valuable discoveries made by those who were not aware of their full, and often most important, significance.

While I am far from being a dianetician (it is not fear of what people might say that prevents me from being one), I have found that dianetics has suggested several new tools that have assisted me in my work with patients. Though the use that I make of these may be considerably at variance with the manner in which they were understood by Hubbard, I do not find it necessary to deny that his was the original idea, and my interest in the development of psychotherapy makes it important that I use this occasion to encourage the serious consideration by others of the significance and possible implications of dianetics.

Certainly, we must consider the provocative suggestion, intended or not, that the dianetic concept of the *engram* has given us relative to the concept of learning. This is a field which has been badly neglected in psychotherapeutic literature. Even where thorough studies have been made, as in dealing with backward children, the subject is largely confined to a study of inadequate orientation, inadequate semantic reactions and inadequate assimilation of reading material. For the most part, it is taken for granted that learning is a process of duration and repetition.

A very large area of learning, however, is characterized by suddenness, either by shock or (if such an expression may be permitted) by a pleasant shock; by what is called in *Gestalt* psychology the "aha" experience. The burned child does not need any training to learn henceforth to avoid the hot stove, and the successful experimenting of the trial and error kind comes with a glow of success and insight of "That's it!"

"This will teach you a lesson" is an expression that shows how well aware we are of the connection of painful experience and learning. The *avoidance* of the painful, e.g., the punishment, becomes a powerful instrument in training.

In psychoanalytical literature this shock learning is called *trauma*, but it is conceived as a mechanical instance, as something that, unrelated to the human organism, descends upon it. The libido and death instinct theory leaves little room— except for "frustration"—for the meaning of the trauma. Dianetics, however, with its concept of *engram*, returns to the more realistic Darwinian theory of individual and race survival and gives trauma a more adequate meaning; at the same time, it supplements the inadequate psychoanalytic formulation of introjection.

In contrast to the otherwise hopelessly bombastic and mechanical terminology of dianetics, the term *engram* seems to be a good one. First, it merely means psycho-physical recording, leaving room for the possibility of beneficial shocks. Secondly, by linking up the survival significance of avoiding *survival-threatening* situations, it is a step towards a truly existentialist theory of psychotherapy.

Another way of learning is by copying, by imitation. If such copying is done unconsciously, psychoanalysis correctly regards this as a process of identification. But by assuming that all unconscious identification is introjection and by omitting the differentiation between identification with somebody's behavior (which is true learning; e.g., in the acquisition of a skill) and identification with somebody's command (which is not learning but submission) as well as by omitting the whole process of assimilation, the whole theory becomes confused. In addition, if the introjected object is, as Freud insists, a love object, then the introjective theory becomes cockeyed. Actually, we introject, we swallow, we avoid tasting and chewing that which we *dislike*, not what we love. Introjects and engrams are foreign bodies in the organism. Both have to be dissolved in order to be assimilated in such a way that they can contribute to the development of the personality.

To complicate matters still further, there is the joy that

some children derive from obeying an adult's commands. This is a form of identification definitely not based upon introjection but rather upon *confluence*.

The essence of introjection is that something is swallowed that remains foreign material in the organism. As it is not assimilated, it can be recovered and redigested; this is an essential part of every successful therapy. Psychoanalysis has not overlooked instances of this sort, which it calls total introjection. A child has been through the painful experience of visiting a dentist; afterwards, he plays at being a dentist with another child as the patient. Why? Because he loves the dentist? Certainly not! And introducing all kinds of auxiliary theories of transference and symbolic father actions in order to squeeze difficult facts into the libido theory is not very useful either.

Here again a piece of the dianetic survival outlook simplifies the theoretical concept. It says that we dramatize the *winning valence;* if we cannot do that, we become sick. Since in the fight for survival, the stronger has the better chance, and in the child's eyes the dentist is stronger than the patient, the identification tends to be with the party in power.

My observations over a long period of time are in accordance with this dianetic insight. The neurotic has a compulsion to vanquish at any price. This has often been recognized as the power drive; Adler and the post-Adlerians have emphasized this. What has not been considered sufficiently is the fact that the patient manipulates the therapist in such a way that he must get the better of him. This manipulation far surpasses in significance the importance of the transference mechanism. Whether he complies or resists, brings dreams that baffle or please; whether he wants to kill or efface himself—somehow he has to get the better of the therapist.

Taking into account this compulsive need for dominance,

obsessional neuroses become easier to cure; they cease to be the bugbear of therapy. One has only to realize that both the *compelling* as well as the *compelled* part of the (equally) split personality want victory. The top-dog part does most of the manipulating by bullying, punishing, etc.; the underdog manipulates by empty promises, procrastination, forgetting, etc.

In the language of dianetics, both parts want to be in the winning valence, thereby bringing the internal war to a stalemate. Or, as Freud expressed it so beautifully, "If you have two servants quarreling, how much work can you expect to be done?" Only here there are no servants quarreling but rather the twin masters themselves.

There is nothing wrong with wanting success and victory, but there is everything wrong with the neurotic victory for the victory's and not for the benefit's sake. Despising the therapist, secretly making a fool of him, rendering him impotent by being stupid, etc., are the favored tools, but such inadequate means don't help the patient to gain victories where he needs them: in his business, over his study material, in his games. Moreover, he has to learn that even without the victory his survival is not dependent upon getting sick, thereby manipulating some "ally" into taking care of him. Briefly, the neurotic does not have the antipoles *health* and *illness* or *victory* and *defeat* but rather a distorted dialectic: the alternatives of *victory* or *illness*.

The main difference between psychoanalysis and dianetics is this: the analyst works, for the most part, with interpretations; that is, with *concepts*, hoping that the thunderbolt of insight may strike home one day and make the patient realize that he is not a child any more, that his wife is not his mother. Dianetics, on the other hand, relies (at least overtly) merely on experience, on *per*ceptual awareness. Thus it has a better chance of rectifying *ad hoc* memories. Actually, dianetics has been as biased as Freudianism in its selection of the material to be processed. By expecting the patient to know Hubbard's book, an unprejudiced experience has been impossible, but the repeater technique, mainly the technique of contacting again and again all the perceptions and emotions, and above all (like Reich) the physical sensations, is of inestimable value. The patient *lives* his unfinished situations and does not merely "talk about" them. Thus he confronts his *alter ego* more effectively than in any other approach. Reich, if he had not been diverted by the compulsive search with microscope and telescope for the hypothetical, unrealistic "Libido" was on the way to developing a truly efficient mode of therapy.

The present book is not for anyone who has a fixation, a complete identification with any of the present day schools. A person with a fixation, as F. M. Alexander and John Dewey have pointed out, will experience everything strange as "wrong"; he will, as I described it, feel hostile to everything outside the ego-boundary. Hubbard, with his mixture of science and fiction, his bombastic way of pretending to something new by giving abstract names (Bouncer, Holder, etc.) to processes, his rejection of responsibility (only what has been done to you counts), his unsubstantiated claims, makes it easy for anyone to reject his work *in toto*, thereby missing any chance to extract any valuable contribution it might contain.

But is dianetics so basically different from the other psychotherapeutic schools? Don't they all, more or less, neglect or talk around the *Self*, its development and creativeness? Does not Freud consider only the intake (introjection) and output (catharsis) of the personality? Is not his Ego a poor something squashed between Super-ego and Id, the role of the self not even being mentioned? And do the more progressive schools deal with much more than the character, or at best, the Ego-concept rather than with the Ego-Functions? Don't they deal even less with the *semantic-integrative* functions of the self?

Likewise, the eclectic will have great difficulty in accepting what is valuable in dianetics. Not having assimilated what he studied, compartmentalizing rather than integrating the different approaches, he might have several fixations instead of one, and which again will prevent him from being unbiased.

Dianetics has swamped this continent and aroused enthusiasm seldom achieved by a book dealing with a psychiatric issue, but the straw-fire burned itself out just as quickly as it began. The discrepancy between claims and fulfillment was too great. And, as always, the revenge after a disappointment is that we forget any good we might have derived from the disappointer.

In this book, Dr. Winter has undertaken the task of salvaging what appears to be valuable in the dianetic effort. The modesty and honesty of the author is very impressive. He tries to come to grips with the essential problem: how can we account for the improvements and even cures that have been achieved with this particular therapy?

First of all, Dr. Winter gives us a detailed description of his technique and his opinions about its efficacy. He leaves open as unconfirmed whether the birth or prenatal experiences are genuine re-experiences, as claimed by Hubbard, or fantasies and projections as others insist.

He introduces the term of *multiordinality of the engram.* This is a valuable formulation, showing that a patient must be made aware of all the perceptual, abstract, symbolic and semantic aspects of a relevant phrase if it is to be effective therapeutically.

Most importantly, he introduces as the therapeutic agent the term of "differentiation," which refers to an act of rational decision asserting that persons or actions were not what

one had "believed" them to be. Thus with Dr. Winter, dianetics develops into a method whereby the irrational—be it
action or thinking (action substitute)—is first experienced
perceptually (along with its pain, obsolescence and insanity),
then by an act of decision condemned as irrational (this is
usually called insight). With this improved orientation a
reorganization of one's actual behavior can be undertaken.

The author disassociates himself from Hubbard's "Everybody can heal Everybody"; he is well aware of the dangers
involved in treatment by unskilled therapists. He knows that
there are all too many neurotics who would treat others for
the very same shortcomings for which they themselves need,
but avoid, treatment.

Unfortunately, the author tends toward excessive specula-
tion. These speculations stand in contrast to the otherwise
careful appreciation of the new approach. They strike me as
premature in part, although they seem valid in others. Furthermore, though Dr. Winter has assimilated much of Korzybski's outlook, he (like Freud and Reich) often mixes the
organism-as-a-whole concept with obsolete concepts of the
mechanistic mentality.

Notwithstanding these limitations, any psychotherapist, if
he can overcome his fixation-bound scoffing (even if he only
tries the repeater technique), will recognize in this book new
tools for therapy. It is true that those who are hopelessly involved in a purely verbal existence will, again with words,
"prove" that all this is nonsense. Or, as they usually formu-
late it: this is all old stuff; what isn't old stuff is wrong. But
for the rest of you, read this book, try now and then a bit of
the technique, but don't call it dianetics, for this would stig-
matize you in the eyes of your confreres. If after a time you
find something useful in this approach, remember that it was
Dr. Winter who braved the storm of condemnation.

We need badly at present the recognition and assimilation of all therapeutic facts in our field; at the same time, we must avoid the dangerous temptation to declare any one of them a panacea. This is true for dianetics as it is for the recovery of the Oedipus Complex, the stabilization of the self-system, the perfection of the orgasm, the dissolving of the character armor, the re-orientation of semantic reactions, the reconciliation of animus and anima, the reconditioning of obsolete reflexes, the complete assimilation of introjects, etc. . . . all these aspects are valuable abstractions of the function of the human being within its environmental field. We have, however, to abstract; that is, to discover many more of these functions to achieve a comprehensive and reliable orientation. Then, and only then, shall we arrive at either a classification of neuroses and specific treatment, or, ideally, at a central theory which will unify facts and treatment without inconsistencies, compartmentalizations or blind-spots.

FREDERICK PERLS, M.D., PH.D.

Los Angeles, May, 1951

——— PREFACE ———

THE PROGRESS of the human race is marked by discoveries. Men observed changes in their surroundings, noticed correlations between these changes and discovered that certain events bore a relationship to other events. With each discovery that was made, it was found that new relationships could be observed—and from this process came Science. Primarily Science was concerned with physical objects and forces external to Man. Medicine as a branch of Science has been preoccupied with the physical body of man; but only in recent years has the mind itself become an object of scientific investigation.

Originally only philosophy and religion dealt with the mind; there were too many variables in this function for the earlier scientists to cope with effectively. Yet the store of knowledge was gradually increased, first by the descriptions of the anatomists, later by the correlations of the physiologists. More recently came the psychonanalysts with their attempts to systematize the knowledge of human mental function.

The search for more knowledge of the human mind goes on constantly, and it is not surprising that such should be the case, for this is perhaps the most fascinating field of all human endeavors. The mind is such a complex affair that there is no dearth of aspects which can be profitably studied.

I have had the opportunity of participating in one of these searches. As will subsequently be told, I made an investigation of a new system of psychotherapy; the originator, L. Ron Hubbard, wrote a book about his therapy and methods and, as a result of my participation in the research, I was asked to write the introduction to his book.

At the time I wrote the introduction I was seriously impressed with the potentialities inherent in Hubbard's hypothesis; I still am. I regard it as unfortunate, however, that he used the manner of presentation which he did, for by so doing he created a great deal of unnecessary criticism and controversy.

Hubbard's book, entitled *Dianetics: The Modern Science of the Mind* (Hermitage House, Inc., New York, 1950), appeared in May of 1950 and shortly thereafter excited an appreciable amount of commotion in the American scene.

Reviews of the book promptly appeared; *Time Magazine* (issue of July 24, 1950) in characteristic fashion referred to dianetics as "the poor man's psychoanalysis; it has a touch of Couéism and a mild resemblance to Buchmanite confession." Another reviewer pointed out that "it so clearly illustrates the most common fallacy of our time in regard to psychological ills . . . . the fallacy of trying to construct a simple science of human behavior based upon mathematics and using for its models the physical sciences and the machine" (Dr. Rollo May in *The New York Times Book Review*, July 2, 1950). Another reviewer called it a dangerous book and gave

ominous warning of what would befall the persons who were
so misled as to try to use Hubbard's methods.

This sort of review was, I feel, inadequate despite the fact
that it was an honest expression of opinion, based on available
data. It was understandable that the reviewers of Hubbard's
book would be misled by the extravagance of style, the absolutistic statements and the failure to give credit to other workers in the field. Critics of scientific writings have been led to
expect that such works will be presented in a sober, judicious
and modest manner—and there was a predictable suspicion of
Dianetics simply because of its literary non-conformity.

A reviewer of a book, after all, has only the book to criticize. He could not be expected to withhold judgment until he
had investigated the truth of the author's statements. A similar
problem confronts the reporter who investigates a new facet
of the American scene (and there were several reports of investigations of dianetics which appeared in national magazines); not being in a position where he can make a judgment
of the value of a therapy, he can only express his opinion of
those who are practicing the therapy. Reporters who investigated the activities of the Hubbard Dianetic Research Foundation were apparently given a poor impression of this organization; their reports were quite harsh, leading the reader to
infer that dianetics was a crackpot pseudo-science, conceived
in charlatanism and nurtured by perfervidly uncritical de-
votees.

However, this is *not* the whole picture; there are numerous facts which reviewers and reporters could not be expected
to know. In my opinion, dianetics is *not* just another fad, completely devoid of merit, appealing only to the psychically weary
and heavy-laden. It has a value—perhaps not so great as its
originator or its enthusiastic adherents wish to believe, but a
definite positive value, nonetheless.

This book was written in order to present the valuable portions of dianetics, which deserve a place in the body of man's knowledge of himself. It seems to me, in all fairness, that it is necessary to expose both sides of the picture to the public gaze; it is especially necessary to acquaint the medical profession with certain previously unknown information about the mind in order that these concepts and methods may be found useful for the betterment of humanity.

There are several facts about the entire dianetics picture which have not yet been made public. It should be known, I believe, that dianetics has been given a careful scrutiny by numerous doctors, psychiatrists, psychoanalysts and psychiatric social workers. I have corresponded with or talked to several hundred of them, and I have found that, when the scientific aspects of dianetics have been honestly examined, they present a real challenge to any serious student of the human mind. Those who have investigated dianetics as a therapeutic technique have found it useful, and are continuing to use it with benefit to their patients. I personally know of a score of psychiatrists who are using a portion of the concepts and techniques of dianetics, and they are unanimous in their feeling that they have acquired a more operational methodology.

And yet these men who are using dianetics do not feel free to admit that they are doing so; they have an understandable hesitancy to call their modifications in technique by the name under which they were first proposed. The reasons for their hesitancy in espousing these methods by name are quite specific, falling into the following categories:

1. They object to the extravagant and unsubstantiated claims made by dianetics—that any intelligent person can practice it, that it is an invariable science, achieving invari-

able results, that a person can become "clear" with a maximum of certainty and a minimum of effort.

2. They object to "the training of lay people without sufficient qualifications." They further feel that in order to deal with the function of the mind one should also have some knowledge of the body.

3. They object to the practice of a healing art by those who have not been ethically oriented by the discipline of professional training, by a sense of true scholarly humility and by awareness of the Hippocratic ideals.

4. They object to the implication that dianetics is the *only* means of treating human ailments, feeling that dianetics can best be used as an adjunct to, rather than as a complete substitute for medical and surgical practices.

These objections are not insuperable—indeed, in a truly scientific presentation of a subject it would be difficult to conceive of such objections ever being made. With appropriate modifications, dianetics has been presented at seminars conducted by myself and members of my group, and its acceptance has increased as its effectiveness has been demonstrated. Its clinical results, while not "invariable" and "precise," appear to represent an improvement in the methods of dealing with disorders of the mind as well as with psychosomatic diseases.

As an example of the attitude of part of the medical profession toward dianetics, I quote from a letter written by a doctor in a mid-western city:

"It is my belief that dianetics has a great place in the field of psychosomatic medicine. This belief is based on experience in the use of dianetic techniques since June, 1950. In one of the first cases, I was astonished to find that attacks of *grand mal* could be turned off and on in an epileptic. . . . . Respiratory infections which are predisposed by psychoneurosis, vertigo, hives, backache, stammering and headaches are but a few of the types of ailments which have yielded under dianetic processing.

"In addition improvement has been shown in homosexuality, paranoid schizophrenia, anxiety neuroses and depressive states. . . .

"In my opinion, dianetics can best be practiced by the medical profession. Its use by the layman should be carefully evaluated, lest the 'amateur' discover he has a psychotic case on his hands. . . . It is not a situation without danger.

"It seems advisable that laymen, in dianetics, avail themselves and their 'pre-clears' [Hubbard's term for "patient"] of physical examinations and psychological surveys by members of the medical profession before undertaking to co-audit [Hubbard's term for mutual exchange of therapy]. Naturally, unless laymen do amateur auditing there would be thousands of cases which could not otherwise be reached, but precaution is advised. My suggestion would be, 'See your doctor before you start auditing.'

"The sociological impact of dianetics can give a vast hope for the future. . . . The medical profession would do well to investigate the potentials of dianetic techniques, concerning itself with research to prove or disprove what dianetics can do. On investigation, it is probable that many physicians will discover their results in the field of psychosomatics will be as startling as the dianetic concept is fantastic."

I believe that the public and the medical profession should know that acceptance of this sort has already occurred, and that scientific dianetics is being used by members of the medical profession with benefit to their patients.

There is another reason why I felt that this book should be written—a reason partaking more of feeling than of fact. The feeling developed during the time I was associated with the

Hubbard Dianetic Research Foundation, when I read and answered the letters inquiring about the medical aspects of dianetics. It was an experience which was both chastening and challenging—chastening because these letters helped to increase my concern with something I have known for a long time: that there is still too much human misery in the world, that the members of the medical profession are still unable to give their patients the care, the knowledge and the understanding which is needed. It is not that the doctors are unwilling to give their patients better care; it is, instead, the paucity of our knowledge which hampers us. As medical men we are in no position to rest upon our laurels; the struggle for human survival has barely begun, and it is still unpredictable whether or not Mankind can retain its precarious advantage.

And yet there is a challenge—a challenge in which those letters were only one voice. We *must,* I believe, take advantage of every opportunity for advancing our abilities to survive, as individuals; as families, as nations, as humans. We must not ignore or deride any new ideas which might possibly help to increase our survival potential.

There are numerous ways in which this is being done, through advances in chemistry, in biology, in electronics, in nuclear physics. It is my conviction that dianetics is sufficiently important to be accorded a place on the agenda of Science and to be investigated until we can ascertain whether or not its actualities will live up to its potentialities.

The manner and style of presentation used in this book were chosen deliberately in order to emphasize that it is the expression of my own opinion, derived from personal observation. I have also, but in a less personal manner, described the methods of applying dianetics as used by myself and my co-workers and fellow-investigators, showing how the methods have been modified and what has resulted from the modifications. Finally, I have endeavored to show what might be done with dianetics and how it can play a part—and, I feel, a useful one—in the efforts of my profession to make this a better world in which to live.

I wish to extend my thanks to my associate, Nancy Roodenburg, for her perceptive suggestions and her painstaking editorial work, to my associate, Myron Beigler, for his assistance and to my many friends whose questions and arguments helped to crystallize the ideas I have tried to express.

I wish also to express my appreciation and respect to L. Ron Hubbard, without whom this book would not have been written.

J. A. W.

New York, N. Y.
May, 1951.

A DOCTOR'S REPORT ON DIANETICS

THE FIRST PHASE

———————— I ————————

In the Spring of 1950 a new book appeared
in the bookstores of the U.S.A. With little advance publicity
and virtually no advertising, it was seized upon by thousands
of readers and within a comparatively short time was high
on the Best Seller list. Its title was *Dianetics: The Modern Science of the Mind* (Hermitage House, Inc., New York); its author a man well-known in science-fiction circles, L. Ron Hubbard.

It is not surprising that a book dealing with the problems of
the functioning of the mind should have a wide popular appeal. For thousands of years man has sought knowledge of the
nature of his own mind; countless words have been written on
the subject, and research goes on constantly in the centers of
learning.

The very fact that so much has been written and that research into mental functioning occupies so much of the attention of many groups of investigators indicates a condition of

1

which most of us are well aware: we are still not completely satisfied with the state of our knowledge.

I happen to be one of those people who is not satisfied with what he knows, but who seeks for a better understanding of the nature of Man and his mind. My chosen profession of medicine has made me keenly aware of the limitations of our present knowledge and has stimulated a desire to find out as much as I can of the causes of human behavior in all of its manifestations. In the years of my medical training and practice I have tried constantly to maintain an awareness of the possibilities for increasing my knowledge.

An apparent opportunity for learning more about human behavior was presented to me in 1949 while I was practicing medicine in Michigan. It was perhaps a set of fortuitous coincidences which led to my being presented with the opportunity; it was no coincidence that I was in a receptive mood for a new idea. For several years after my graduation from medical school I had been engaged in the general practice of medicine; as part of my basic personal orientation towards medicine I felt it was important for me to know my patients as people, rather than as cases of illness. I found it necessary to help my patients with their troubles as well as their physical ailments, and I should have been pathologically unobservant not to have noted how a person's manner of going about the business of living affected his resistance to disease and his abilities to recover.

My avocations, too, had played a part in my introduction to what is now known as dianetics. For several years I had written articles on medical subjects for the laity, and some of my work had been published in *Astounding Science Fiction*, a magazine edited by John W. Campbell, Jr. Despite its fanciful title, this publication is one which has a wide appeal to the scientifically-trained persons; 80% of its readers are college graduates, and among its contributors are well-known doctors, chemists, engineers, physicists and astronomers.

In July, 1949 I received a long letter from Mr. Campbell, in which he told me of some investigations in which he thought I might be interested. He told me that "L. Ron Hubbard, who happens to be an author, has been doing some psychological research. . . . He's gotten important results. His approach is, actually, based on some very early work of Freud's, some work of other men, and a lot of original research. He's not a professional psychoanalyst or psychiatrist . . . . . he's basically an engineer. He approached the problem of psychiatry from the heuristic viewpoint—to get results. . . . . The following are conclusions he's derived.

"Basically, Hubbard finds, all psychological troubles stem from a situation somewhere containing the following simple elements:

1. Strong *physical* pain.
2. A powerful threat (real or so believed by the organism) to the survival of the organism.
3. A non-analytic state of the brain. This—and only this— type of situation will implant a psychological jam which he calls an 'Impediment.'

"The important thing, he finds, is that most serious psychological jams stem from some basic painful, dangerous experience when the subject was *unconscious* or incapable of *conscious, analytic thought.*

"The important part of the unconscious experience is this: the analytical, evaluational functions of the mind *are not in gear.* A statement made under those circumstances is accepted timelessly, and without evaluation for truth, reasonableness, or anything else. Here's the sort of thing that happens:

"An amputee veteran, with loss of one foot and slight impairment of one hand is in a hopeless despondency condition

—just can't adjust. The psychiatrist takes him back to the war experience with sodium pentothal, back to the time the mortar shell got him. Pain, and plenty of it—badly smashed left arm and leg, a number of painful, but relatively minor wounds of body and face on that side. Makes him look like a bloody mess, though. They take him through, to the period when he passed out, and pick up again when he recovered consciousness in the aid station. Doesn't seem to clear him up. He still insists he'd be better off dead.

"Hubbard took him through, through the shell burst, and *through the period of unconsciousness*. That's when it happened. A medic had come along, seen him and another injured man, said, 'This guy's hopeless—he's better off dead anyway. We'll take that man there.' A second medic team had brought the patient in; he was badly injured, but nowhere near as bad as he looked.

"With the conscious mind out of circuit, a man loses the power of evaluation, but not the power of memory. But he reacts on a lower-animal basis. The stimulus is intense pain, acute danger—and the calculating machine in the skull, half a billion years ago, was designed to permit mammals to learn to avoid danger. It classifies and remembers all associated circumstances—not all *relevant* circumstances—as part of the danger incident, and reacts powerfully to it. It's a timeless thing, too; the statement 'He's better off dead anyhow' would, in a conscious mind, be interpreted as 'He appears from here, and right now, as though he might be better off dead,' and a conscious mind would evaluate and reject it. The unconscious mind can't evaluate. But it records with the accuracy and permanence of a phonograph."

This was an interesting concept, to say the least. I had never before heard anyone advance the idea that a person could be affected psychically during periods of unconscious-

ness. During all my years as a doctor I had never considered
—nor had anyone else ever suggested to my knowledge—that
a patient who was unconscious by reason of injury or anesthesia might be partially aware of what was going on. Medical
knowledge, for the most part, assumed that a person who was
unconscious or anesthetized was incapable of all except the
vegetative functions—certainly not the function of memory.

I answered Mr. Campbell's letter and requested more information on Hubbard's work. Within a short time another
long letter arrived, elaborating on the reactions to this sort of
therapy and discussing some of the implications of the aberrative effects of information received during unconsciousness.
He concluded by saying that "these things are unexplored
byways just indicated vaguely by the solid work Hubbard has
actually done. There is only one important statistical fact
that I think should be dealt with. This has been research; Hubbard has been working on it as a research program, trying to
find out what causes what, and how to fix it. Therefore, with
cooperation from some institutions, some psychiatrists, he has
worked on all types of cases. Institutionalized schizophrenics,
apathies, manics, depressives, perverts, stuttering, neuroses
—in all, nearly 1000 cases. But just a brief sampling of each
type; he doesn't have proper statistics in the usual sense.
But he has one statistic. He has *cured every patient* he worked.
He has cured ulcers, arthritis, asthma."

My first response to this information was one of polite in-
credulity. How could it be that a man without any medical
training could get results which doctors had rarely, if ever,
been able to obtain? Notwithstanding, I thought of the times
when medical knowledge had been increased by contributions
from non-medical practitioners—how Withering learned of
the medicinal properties of the purple fox-glove from an old
woman in the country, how the science of microscopy was

advanced by a Dutch janitor, how the technique of retino-scopy was developed by a postmaster. Could this idea of Hubbard's be another non-medical contribution to medical advancement?

I became aware again of the perplexity which plagues all doctors—the "why" of human behavior. I thought of all the questions which had gone unanswered or which had been answered in a tentative or equivocal manner—of questions which were frequently unasked because of their presumed unanswerability. Why did Mr. M. attempt to commit suicide? Why was it that Mrs. E. began to hear voices telling her to kill her new-born baby? Why did an intelligent man like Mr. P. find it necessary to drink a quart of whiskey every day? Why did Mrs. T. have coronary occlusion?

The list of questions beginning with "why" could be ex-tended indefinitely. They all had one element in common: I knew of no satisfactory answer for any of them. The "an-swers" and explanations which I had learned in medical school and which I passed on to my patients were superficial, taking into account only the preceding link in the chain of causality. A patient would ask me, "Why does a person get coronary occlusion?" and I would answer glibly, "Because there is a narrowing of the lumen of the coronary arteries." And with that answer he would appear to be satisfied.

I was not satisfied with that sort of answer, however, nor did I find the explanations of "familial predilections" and "lowered resistance" to be operational. An explanation for the causation of a disease would, if it were satisfactory, in-clude the means of treating that disease. If one explained typhoid fever as a punishment inflicted by a malign Fate or a whim of the gods, there was no rational treatment; when it was found to be a water-borne infection, the medical pro-fession could do something to prevent it.

I was of the opinion, moreover, that questions of causation of illness could be answered only if one had a holistic view of the patient. To consider diabetes as a disease of the pancreas led one into a therapeutic *cul-de-sac*—one could treat this condition only by substitutional means, giving the patient the hormone which he apparently lacked. But what about the woman, previously healthy, who developed a severe case of diabetes shortly after her husband committed suicide? The bullet which ended her husband's life certainly did not injure her pancreas—but she behaved as if it did.

In my past efforts to regard a person as a whole organism I had become interested in endocrinology, taking the viewpoint that the endocrine system was a means of integrating a person's total response to environmental stresses. I found that a man who could not think clearly, who was nervous and irritable, could be helped to a more effectual way of living by giving him androgenic substances, that a woman who nagged her husband might cease doing so if she was given a sufficient amount of estrogen. Some of my results were good, but I was well aware that they were limited. I could not predict with any degree of accuracy how effectual my methods would be, nor could I forecast how long any benefits would persist. I found, moreover, that I could get endocrine-like effects merely by giving counsel and advice; helping a person to resolve a dilemma by open and friendly discussion was often as effectual as a hypodermic injection of a hormone.

I had spent a year in part-time research at the University of Illinois in an effort to increase my knowledge of the human-as-a-whole, but found instead a tendency in academic circles toward further compartmentalization of the patient, with the holistic viewpoint conspicuous for its absence. I had become interested in General Semantics, too—and while I agreed with Korzybski that "the word is not the object," I found no satisfactory explanation for how such a confusion between levels of abstraction had arisen in the first place.

Because of my eclecticism it was not difficult for me to decide that Hubbard's ideas deserved more than a casual dismissal; to ignore them might be depriving my chosen profession of a possibly valuable methodology. I therefore communicated with Hubbard and suggested that he present his ideas to the medical profession for their consideration. I told him that I had some friends in Chicago, well-known in the psychiatric field, who might be interested in examining his results and testing his methods.

I received a courteous reply, in which he said that he was "preparing, instead of a rambling letter, an operator's manual for your use. . . . Certainly appreciate your interest. My vanity hopes that you will secure credit to me for eleven years of unpaid research, but my humanity hopes above that that this science will be used as intelligently and extensively as possible, for it *is* a science and it does produce exact results uniformly and can, I think, be of benefit."

I had also suggested that he attempt to publish some of his findings in some lay magazine as a means of stimulating interest in his work; to this he replied, "The articles you suggest would be more acceptable coming from another pen than mine."

The manual eventually arrived; in the letter which accompanied it Hubbard said, "That I spent eleven years on this should not be very surprising. I am, after all, a trained mathematician and studied my theory of equations very well. . . . The work in Abnormal Dianetics is up now to the state where it can be effectively applied broadly with exactly predictable results and uniform success. . . . If a good operator works on any patient 'sane' or 'insane' not physically

neurasthenic he will get 100 out of 100 'clears.' * There aren't
any 'special cases' save in the diagnosis and initial entrance
where an operator has to use his wits against one of these
'Self-preserving' impediments. A very exhaustive research
has located no exception to any axiom and broad application
to types has discovered no exception to treatment technique
—anything surrenders.

"No existing case histories are of use to the dianetic re-
searcher as they lack the essential data and no existing neurotic or psychotic classification has been found to have any
meaning in dianetic practice or diagnosis. So it's a clean
slate. . . . Every field (psycho-analysis, hypnotism, Christ-
ian Science, etc.) I investigated had 10,000 wrong [answers]
for every right one."

I must confess to a slight feeling of perturbation at the
apparently absolutistic viewpoint which Mr. Hubbard's letter
implied. I had become accustomed to a more guarded expression of one's views, to an orientation based on statistical
probability rather than invariability. Yet I realized that enthusiasm for one's work was a prerequisite for continuing
effort, and I did not wish to permit my own conservatism to
prejudice my efforts to learn more of Hubbard's ideas.

Several copies were made of the manual which Hubbard
had sent: two of them were sent to colleagues of mine in
Chicago. Both of them expressed interest in the ingenuity of
the ideas, but they were strongly sceptical of the efficacy
of the method. I concluded from their comments that neither
of them planned to make any further investigation.

In spite of their negative reactions I decided to continue

* "Clear": the state postulated by Hubbard as resulting from dianetic therapy; in a sense, the goal of dianetic therapy. This concept is discussed at
greater length later in this book.

with my study of the manual and I attempted to apply the
technique to one of my patients who had a rather bizarre
illness, apparently psychosomatic, which had been diagnosed
as an atypical form of epilepsy. My attempts to produce
Hubbard's results were unsuccessful with her; when I queried
him about it, he stated that I was working with a late-life
incident instead of looking for the basic causation in very
early—possibly prenatal—life.

There were numerous times when I was tempted to dismiss
the entire concept as an ingenious but ineffectual ideal and
to concentrate my efforts on the practice of conventional
medicine, but one of the phases of my practice intervened.
I was doing some work for the Probate Court which, in Michigan, has jurisdiction over the insane and the juvenile delin-
quents. In this capacity I was called on to examine a variety
of people who presented problems of maladjustment to society
and to recommend whether or not they should be committed
to a state institution for care and treatment. During the process
of examining these maladjusted people I had numerous opportunities for discussing the social problem of the misfit
with those who specialized in this field. The judges, the psychiatrists and the social workers with whom I talked were
unanimous both in expressing a dissatisfaction with present
social methodologies and in feeling rather hopeless about
improving their methods. When I discussed Hubbard's ideas
with them, I observed a limited sort of enthusiasm, which
might be expressed as, "That would be nice if it worked;
you try it out and then tell me about it." In other words, my
attempts to interest them in an investigation of dianetics met
with verbal encouragement but a dearth of actual cooperation.

There was, as I saw it, only one conclusion to be drawn
at that time: if anyone in medicine were to investigate dianetics, it would have to be myself. I also concluded that expo-

sition by correspondence alone would not teach me to use dianetic techniques, but that I would have to observe it in action.
I thereupon made arrangements to spend a week or so in
New Jersey, where Hubbard was living at the time. He had
very hospitably invited me to stay at his home, and he told
me that I would have the chance to observe his technique,
apply it to patients and undergo the therapy myself, if I so
desired.

I arrived in Bay Head, N.J. on October 1, 1949, and immediately became immersed in a life of dianetics and very
little else. I observed two of the patients whom Hubbard had
under treatment at this time, and spent hours each day in
watching him send these men "down the time-track." After
some observation of the reactions of others, I concluded that
my learning of this technique would be enhanced by sub-
mitting myself to therapy. I took my place on the couch,
spending an average of three hours a day trying to follow
the directions for recalling "impediments." The experience
was intriguing; I found that I could remember much more
than I had thought I could, and I frequently experienced the
discomfort which is now known as "restimulation." While
listening to Hubbard "running" one of his patients, or while
being "run" myself, I would find myself developing unac-
countable pains in various portions of my anatomy, or becoming extremely fatigued and somnolent. I had nightmares of
being choked, of having my genitalia cut off, and I was convinced that dianetics as a method could produce effects.

I observed that these periods of discomfort were apt to
precede a session wherein my depth of insight was increased,
and I therefore developed a tolerance of my own discomfort
—an attribute which had previously been absent. The idea
that discomfort heralded relief and insight seemed encouraging to me.

I felt, in general, that I was obtaining some benefits from Hubbard's methods of therapy; I was also aware of the possible inaccuracies of a subjective evaluation of my own progress; I therefore endeavored to make up for this by observing the other patients closely. It was possible during this short period of observation to note only the differences in their behavior before and after each therapy session. The changes were obvious: before a session I would see agitation, depression and irritability; after a session the patient would be cheerful and relaxed.

One day I was amazed to observe one of the patients go into a period of uncontrollable laughter; he had gone into his therapy that day looking quite depressed and withdrawn, and the material he brought up that session seemed to be quite unremarkable. Suddenly, on recalling a phrase, he began to laugh heartily and kept it up for well over an hour. The laughter was so prolonged and could be re-excited by such trivia that I suspected either an acute mania or a hebephrenia. I mentioned this to Hubbard, who told me that he had observed this phenomenon frequently in the past, and that it was characteristic of every case in which there had been much fear or terror. It was as if the phrase which the person had recalled carried a terrifying threat and the realization of the essential silliness of equating fear with words brought forth the laughter. Other than this he offered no theoretical explanation for the phenomenon. The patient's laughter subsided after a while and he seemed none the worse for it.

After three weeks my wife came from Michigan to visit me. In this relationship I had an opportunity to compare my reactions and attitudes of that time with my pre-dianetic state. I felt that my capacity for communicating with her had improved, and I now seemed capable of feeling and expressing a depth of affection which I had never experienced before.

During her stay she observed several sessions of my therapy and of the therapy of the other patients and familiarized herself with the major points of technique. I tried my abilities with this new therapy on her, and observed the signs of the state which is now known as "reverie"—the fluttering eyelids, the deepening of respiration, the lessened awareness of the present environment. I was, of course, aware of certain similarities between this and the hypnotic state; however, certain features also appeared to distinguish it. My wife reported that the repetition of certain phrases would elicit discomfort in various parts of her body, and that continued repetition of the phrase would be associated with a decrease in the intensity of the discomfort.

After a week's visit she returned home, while I stayed on in Bay Head, determined to continue with my investigation of dianetics. My evaluation of it continued to be ambivalent. I felt certain that the technique was effectual, at least; by application of dianetic principles certain effects could be produced. These effects, so far as I could determine, had never before been observed, although certain aspects were known. Investigators from Freud up to Flanders Dunbar had long since demonstrated one or another type of association of words with illness. For example, it had been known that a patient might feel pain in his neck region because his wife was "a pain in the neck" to him, and that adjustment of the marital conflict would sometimes relieve the patient of his pain. I knew of no work, however, where an effect was produced in which a person would develop a pain in the neck following the repetition of a phrase, and would have the pain disappear on further repetition. This specific cause and effect relationship between words and dysfunction was new —and it appeared to offer a means of manipulating the function of the mind in a manner which had never been known before.

There was much to be said in favor of dianetics: there were also some points which could be criticized. For one thing, my training in medicine and my studies in General Semantics made me extremely hesitant to accept broad generalizations and absolutistic statements; I was oriented toward a reality based on statistical probability, rather than a two-valued logic. The philosophy of dianetics, as it was propounded to me, seemed to abound in the type of concepts which I tended always to question. The possibility of alternative explanations for these phenomena also kept coming to my mind.

A careful recapitulation of what I had learned led me to conclude the following: here were some observations which appeared to me to be original and a hypothesis which offered a tentatively acceptable explanation. The observations could not be explained in any conventional psychologic theory that I knew of; ergo, dianetics at least warranted further investigation.

My therapy continued; I went through the experience of being terror-stricken at the idea of recalling my grandmother's death and finding this terror dissolve in sobbing and weeping when I reviewed a childhood scene in which I was first told about what happens when a person dies. I saw the others experience a similar emotional discharge or release of affect during the recounting of comparable situations, and saw how terror would be followed by weeping, the tears being succeeded by an attitude of cheerful acceptance, which might be expressed as, "Well, I understand this now. What's next?"

I returned to Michigan for a few days visit at Thanksgiving and found that my six-year-old son was having difficulties. A few weeks previously he had gone to a high-school play in which one of the characters was a ghost, dressed in the usual white sheet. That night he developed a fear of the dark, and refused to go upstairs alone, demanding that all the lights be turned on. I asked him why he should be afraid of the dark; his reply was, "That's where the ghosts are."

"Why should you be afraid of ghosts?" I asked.

He looked at me with a very serious and tremulous gaze and said, "They choke you."

I remembered that when he was born he had had considerable difficulty. There was a premature separation of the placenta, and it had been necessary to perform a version and extraction to deliver him. My wife had also told me that he had shown evidences of respiratory dysfunction immediately after birth. This gave me an idea of a possible cause of his present fears, so I had him lie down and close his eyes. I began the counting procedure which was used at the time to assist a patient into the process of recall.

I suggested, "Let's go to the first time you saw a ghost. Can you see him?"

"Yup."

"What does he look like?"

"He has on a long white apron, a little white cap on his head and a piece of white cloth over his mouth."

I noticed at this time that his respirations were labored, and that he twisted and squirmed on the couch as if agitated.

"What's the ghost's name?" I asked.

"Bill S . . ." he answered.

It was the name of the obstetrician who had delivered him. I had him look at the "ghost" a few more times, and as he did so I observed that his respiratory rate gradually decreased, that the generalized tension was replaced by a more relaxed attitude and that his agitated squirming diminished markedly. When the maximum relaxation had apparently been obtained after ten or twelve recountings, I told him to open his eyes. It has been over a year since that short session with my son, and he has not had a recurrence of his fear of the dark in all that time.

My wife and I had numerous discussions about the validity of our son's recollection and have tried to determine if he could have acquired this information by some other channel. We are certain of the following: he never saw Dr. S. dressed in a surgical cap and gown except at the moment of delivery; he has never been told that there was any respiratory difficulty associated with his birth. To the best of our knowledge he has never seen Dr. S. since leaving the hospital at the age of two weeks. It is also interesting to note that Dr. S. is a schoolmate of mine, and is therefore called by his first name rather than his title; it would seem therefore that my son was unaware that "Bill" was also a doctor, and that therapeutic benefits were obtained without the realization of the role which "Bill S." played in his life. I can offer no explanation of why my son brought up the name "Bill S." instead of "Dr. S."; the fact remains that that is what he said.

I feel, however, that the validity of this data is of secondary importance; I am not trying to adduce "proof" so much as I am desirous of demonstrating the efficacy of the method.

On my return to New Jersey after Thanksgiving I continued with my therapy by Hubbard and also did some preliminary work on a presentation of dianetics to the medical profession. Nomenclature proved to be a prime obstacle to expressing the concepts of this new method of approach to mental illnesses. Hubbard had used the word "impediment" as a label for the moment of pain, unconsciousness and threat to survival which he believed resulted in aberration of the patient's behavior. We (Hubbard, Campbell and I) felt that this word should be discarded because it was too long and might be confused with other usages, such as an impediment in one's speech.

After considerable discussion we concluded that terminology should be revised with the following criteria kept in mind: older terminology or terminology from other medical fields should be avoided, because the acceptance of a term from a certain school of thought might imply acceptance of the tenets of that school of thought. Rather than create a confusion between the Freudian "unconscious" and the dianetic concept of unconsciousness, we would coin a new term. Secondly, words in common usage might be associated with pain in the minds of some patients, and should therefore be avoided. Finally, some of the concepts of dianetics could not be expressed accurately in the words we had at our disposal. For example, we deal with "memories" which are not easily recallable—how then were we to refer to these? We might have referred to "forgotten past experiences," but that term would have been unwieldy as well as incorrect, as the patient acted as if he never forgot these traumatic events. While the Freudian term of "repressed memory" was recognized to be somewhat parallel, it was discarded because of the somewhat different approach of dianetics both in theory and methodology.

Several alternatives were suggested. The phenomenon of less-than-complete-consciousness was called *anaten,* a condensation of the words "analyzer attenuation." What had been called an "impediment" was now called a *norn,* the name for the Norse goddesses of Fate, who controlled Man's destiny and made him follow a course of conduct *nolens volens.* These terms were used in the article by Hubbard which appeared in the May, 1950 issue of *Astounding Science Fiction;* this was the first appearance in print of the subject *Dianetics.*

I attempted another approach to the problem of terminology, using the conventional medical scheme of constructing neologisms from Greek roots. As a substitute for "impediment" I proposed the word *comanome*, from "coma" meaning unconsciousness and "nomos" meaning law. A "comanome," therefore, was both an unconscious law and a law of unconsciousness. Instead of calling it "unconsciousness" I used the word *allocoma*, another type of unconsciousness, to point up the difference between the usual and the dianetic sense of the word.

Further discussion led to dissatisfaction with all three words, and it was finally decided to use the term *engram*, which is defined by Dorland as "a lasting mark or trace. The term is applied to the definite and permanent trace left by a stimulus in the protoplasm of a tissue. In psychology it is the lasting trace left in the psyche by anything that has been experienced psychically; a latent memory picture." * It should be noted that this term was *not* borrowed from Semon, as some have suggested. At the time this term was chosen, Semon's work was unknown to our group.†

A paper, using the terminology of Greek derivation, and giving a brief resumé of the principles and methodology of dianetic therapy, was prepared and submitted informally to one of the editors of the *Journal* of the American Medical Association. The editor informed me that the paper as written did not contain sufficient evidence of efficacy to be acceptable and was, moreover, better suited to one of the journals which dealt with psychotherapy. A revision of this paper, together with some case histories given me by Hubbard, was submitted to the *American Journal of Psychiatry*; it was refused, again on the grounds of insufficient evidence.

Dorland's Medical Dictionary, 17th ed., W. B. Saunders Co., Philadelphia, 1936.
†Semon, Richard, *Mnemic Psychology*. George Allen & Unwin, Ltd., London, 1923.

During this time there was considerable discussion among us as to the theory of valence. It had been observed that when a person acted in an aberrated manner, he usually used a set of stock phrases which were often not quite appropriate to the situation. He might also use little mannerisms, such as a cough or a throat-clearing or a scratching of the head, as an accompaniment to his less-than-ideal conduct. It was suggested that these mannerisms and phrases had been used by the person from whom the patient had learned the response-pattern, and that the patient was assuming the role or *valence* of the person he was emulating. It was further observed in therapy that a patient might not recall a situation from his own viewpoint, but could recall it more easily if he was permitted to take the viewpoint, or valence, of the most successful person in the situation.

With further observations, it was frequently discovered that some patients acted as if they were completely unable to recall their own sensations and emotions during a painful episode; instead, they identified themselves with and dramatized the behavior of this other successful person—or "winning valence," as Hubbard called it. It became rather obvious that a good deal of aberrated behavior was characterized by such dramatizations. It also became evident that the more of these dramatizations were uncovered and the events approached in dianetic therapy, the less need the person had to adopt them in a behavioral sense; as a result, he was better able to experience his own reality, or, as Hubbard put it more mechanistically, "enter his own valence."

I returned to my home in Michigan again over the Christmas holidays. During that time I gave numerous demonstrations of dianetic technique to my friends. This was the first opportunity I had had to work with anyone who had not had previous experience with dianetics. The event I chose to investigate for demonstration purposes was birth, which I felt was sufficiently dramatic to make an impression on people who were certain that they couldn't recall anything which had happened to them before the age of three. My subjects responded as predicted; they developed the characteristic headache, certain appropriate phrases occurred to them, and the headache decreased on repetition of the phrases.

I was rather surprised to find out that two of my friends developed upper respiratory infections about three days after the demonstration in which they had taken part. One case was sufficiently severe to necessitate this person's being absent from work for several days. This succession of events led me to wonder if dianetics was quite so harmless as I had been led to believe.

While at home, I came to the decision that I would no longer be content to practice medicine as I had done before. One of the phases of medical practice which had always been baffling to me was the difficulty in predicting the reaction of a patient to a given form of therapy. With dianetics the predictability of results appeared to be extremely high. Moreover, the potentialities inherent in the philosophy of dianetics were so great that I felt challenged to do all I could to help them develop into actualities. The practice of medicine was, I thought, bound to be affected in a constructive fashion. I wanted to be able to assist in the task of making dianetics a useful tool in the hands of the medical profession, and I knew that I would not be content until I had acquired much more experience in the use of the technique. I also felt that certain aspects of the hypothesis needed revision or clarification, and I was anxious to study this aspect.

I returned to New Jersey long enough to find a home for my family, then returned to Michigan, sold my office equipment and with my wife and children left for our new home.

Soon after I had established my home in New Jersey I acquired a patient who had previously had some dianetic therapy in an attempt to be relieved of a state of chronic terror. Physical examination showed that she was otherwise in good health, her difficulties being mainly psychic. She reported that the results which had been obtained from therapy had been but slight. On further questioning I discovered that she had spoken a foreign language until the age of five, and that she had neglected to give this information to her former therapist. When therapy was resumed, the language factor was taken into account; in the recounting of early "engrams" the words were repeated in the language in which they had been originally spoken. There was soon a noticeable improvement in her status; she became much less fearful and was able to join in social gatherings with greater ease.

This was an extremely interesting observation to me: it offered suggestive evidence in proof of the theory that these extra-conscious "memories" were recorded as sounds and not as meaningful words.

By this time Hubbard had begun to write his book and was so immersed in his labors that I had little opportunity to see him. He had decided, I knew, to write a book directed toward the laity rather than at the medical profession; he felt that professional interest in dianetics would be stimulated more rapidly by first informing the public, then having the public urge their doctors to find out more about the techniques of the new therapeutic approach.

The article which was to appear in *Astounding Science Fiction* had been completed and was scheduled for publication. Mr. Campbell had informed his readers of the forthcoming article, and some inquiries were already beginning to be made by interested readers.

One inquiry came from a young man who was a student

in a professional school in New York City. His wife, he said, had been in the hospital since the first of the year suffering with an intractable case of diarrhea. He had been told by her attending physician that the prognosis was a gloomy one, and that there was a strong probability that she would not survive for longer than a month. A vagotomy had been contemplated, but the surgeon hesitated to recommend it because of the girl's unfavorable condition.

The husband was desperate and was willing to try anything which offered any hope for his wife. After making inquiries of Mr. Campbell he was referred to me and he asked me to see his wife; I agreed, warning him that I could give him no assurances as to the outcome, although I did not feel that she could be harmed.

I first saw the patient in New York. The hospital was one of those connected with one of the medical schools—a so-called "teaching hospital." The patient's husband had received permission from the attending physician for me to see her in consultation; consequently, there were no delays or obstacles placed in my way.

The chart showed that she had been admitted on January 16, weighing 82¾ pounds; during the period of hospitalization her weight had fluctuated, the high being 87, the low being 80½ pounds. On the day I first saw her, March 19, she weighed 81½. Her stools averaged 11 to 14 per diem.

A thorough physical examination, including X-rays, blood chemistry and bacteriologic examinations of the stools, had revealed no clues to the cause of her difficulties. The provisional diagnosis at this time was "Diarrhea due to disturbed small intestinal function; etiology unknown. Possible nontropical sprue or regional enteritis."

Her treatment had consisted of high caloric feedings, high

vitamin intake, folic acid, liver extract *per hypo* and banthine —a drug which acts as a vagal paralysant. She had apparently made no response to these medications and a progress note on the chart stated that the patient was "an extremely difficult problem of management. Response to medical therapy and psychotherapy has varied but she has become steadily worse (wt. now 80—1 yr. ago 120). Feel that . . . we are forced to have vagotomy performed." Nurses' notes carried such observations as "Extremely discouraged—not interested in anything."

The chart also carried a note by the physician who had been concerned with the psychiatric aspects of her case. I quote the note *in toto*:

"Psychosomatic consultation 17 January 1950.

"Pt. has been seen in Psychosomatic and Psychoanalytic Clinics intermittently from October 1948 to present time. The clinical course of illness has been stormy with marked improvement initially followed by gradual exacerbation starting July 1949. This is an obsessive-compulsive girl with disorganizing behavior verging on psychotic that has been present for at least 15 years.

"Somatic symptoms started six years ago at the time of her mother's death. These have been primarily related to the gastro-intestinal tract, and include globus hystericus, duodenal ulcer, regional ileitis and mucous colitis. Obviously the psychiatric prognosis is limited, in view of the severity and duration of her illness, but it should be noted that severe neurotic behavior preceded her somatic complaints by many years. Consequently, any alleviation of her present gastro-intestinal symptoms would necessitate further psychiatric care of the concomitant emotional problems. Should the present somatic complaints disappear following medical and surgical treatment, others would inevitably follow without competent psychiatric guidance.

"There is an immediate and serious problem involving progressive loss of weight and general debilitation which intensive psychotherapy has been unable to arrest. Decision as to surgical intervention should rest solely on evaluation of present physical status, as further deterioration in her health may make surgery at later date impossible."

Such was the opinion of her physicians when I first saw her. I made no attempt at physical examination, merely noting that she was thin and emaciated and that her complexion was sallow and marked by numerous acniform papules. She seemed weak and listless, and it was necessary to use a wheel-chair to transport her to the room in which I was to make my attempt at dianetic therapy.

I did not try to indoctrinate her in the terminology of dianetics, merely asking her to lie down and relax with closed eyes. She was instructed not to try to "remember" anything, but simply to tell me whatever thoughts occurred to her without attempting to evaluate them.

I first asked her to consider her illness and to think about her dysentery, then asked her to give me the first word which flashed into her mind. She replied, "Dirty." I asked her to repeat the word and to go back to a time when someone was saying it to her.

"Dirty . . . dirty . . . dirty . . . that's funny! I can hear my mother saying it to me."

I asked her to answer my next question with the first number that occurred to her; then abruptly asked, "How old are you?"

"Six."

"Six what?"

"Six weeks. That's silly. I couldn't possibly be able to remember anything at that time."

It was again pointed out that she should make no attempt to evaluate the validity of her responses but to accept them as just that—responses. She was then asked to continue to repeat the word "dirty."

She interrupted her repetition after a few seconds by saying, "My mother is spanking me; I can feel it and it hurts!"

She continued to repeat the word, then amplified it to the phrase, "You're always dirty." A few more repetitions and she yawned; when asked about the discomfort in the gluteal region, she remarked that it had disappeared.

In this fashion I worked with her for about two hours, touching on such incidents as her witnessing an attack in which her mother had suffered a cerebral hemorrhage. She reported that she had screamed at the doctor, "Do something!" Another incident was reported wherein her father was complaining, "Everybody else gets what they want; all I get is shit."

She was quite reluctant to verbalize this four-letter vulgarism; from the distortion of her features and the writhing on the couch one could infer that the word caused her violent discomfort. After ten or fifteen repetitions of the phrase her agitation subsided; a few more recountings and the words in the phrase "lost their meaning." At the end of the session she said she felt well, although slightly fatigued.

I saw her again six days later. Her hospital chart showed that she had had no bowel movements on the day following the first session, and that during the next five days she averaged only seven stools per diem. She had also gained two pounds in weight. Nurses' notes carried the comments "more cheerful" and "very cheerful." The only change in medication in the interim was a transfusion of 500 cc. of whole blood on the third day following the first dianetic session.

The ensuing two hours of therapy was a continuation of the previous session. She reviewed incidents of being upset and disturbed by her mother's insisting that she take a laxative, with the admonition, "Take your medicine—it'll make your bowels move." There were other incidents in which both her mother and grandmother had said, "You always have dirty pants." Finally the patient reported a sensation of intense generalized pressure; when asked what she thought was happening, she said, "It seems as if my mother is having a bowel movement." An inquiry about the words associated with this pressure-sensation elicited the phrase, "What a relief!"

I had her repeat this experience at least forty times. I asked her to become aware of the pressure-sensation, then to repeat the words, "What a relief." With each recounting the discomfort of the pressure lessened; the patient became sleepy for a minute or so, then yawned and stretched. After about twenty-five repetitions she became annoyed at having to repeat the words, then became indifferent and finally laughed at the words because "they're so silly." A few more repetitions and she was apparently unable to remember what the words were; it was as if she had completely forgotten them.

Two days later she was dismissed from the hospital, feeling quite well and rapidly recovering her strength. Within a week she was able to walk for at least a mile without becoming fatigued. The diarrhea had completely stopped, and she began to gain weight, gaining 20 pounds in six weeks.

Her present status, approximately 14 months after her initial contact with dianetics, is a favorable one. She appears to be maintaining a normal weight and is able to pursue social activities without observable difficulties.

I was very much pleased with the results this girl seemed to obtain from dianetic therapy. I did not regard these results as a permanent cure—and subsequent developments suggest that dianetics as practiced at that time did not necessarily obtain "cures." What was important to me was that a psychotherapeutic technique produced immediate results in a case which was refractory to usual medical and psychiatric measures. The use of a type of treatment based on a hypothesis of mental function had been effectual in halting a process which was rapidly leading towards death.

In other words, here was a hypothesis by which we could manipulate and predict events. The hypothesis was partially correct, at least, or these results would not have been obtained. The next job was to find out about the exceptions to this hypothesis, the zones in which it did not work—to test it, as rigorously as possible.

Another patient whom I was treating at this time was a woman whose chief complaints were "nervousness," tremor and fear of being among people. She responded to dianetic therapy in the manner observed by Hubbard: she would "return" to an incident, feel some discomfort and some words would occur to her. On repeating the words, the discomfort would lessen, the words would be modified, she would become annoyed, then indifferent, then would laugh about the silliness of the verbal content and would seem to forget what she had just said. On reviewing a scene in which she had experienced some painful emotion, she would weep copiously; with further recounting she would weep less and would finally become quite cheerful about an event which previously she had preferred to avoid.

She was under treatment for about three weeks, having an average of three hours of therapy a day. She improved to some extent, but not so much as I had expected. Her improvement, I felt, could have been credited as much to the difference in environment as it could to the therapy which she had been receiving, although she reported that she had changed her environment in the past without noticeable benefits.

I had also tried to teach this patient some of the technique of dianetic therapy, as she had expressed her intention of working with her husband on her return home. Hubbard had claimed (he also has expressed this claim in his book) that virtually anyone could practice dianetics; a little training in the technique and the underlying principles and any intelligent person could become an "auditor," as he decided to term the therapist. The few observations I had made up until this time had not led me to disagree; in fact I was most interested in the possibilities consequent to this contention. One of the great objections to previous psychotherapies was that it was available to only those fortunate few who could afford the fees necessarily charged by a psychiatrist or analyst. If dianetics could be practiced by anyone, it would be available to all—perhaps this could be the beginning of a Golden Age of greater sanity.

My efforts to teach this patient how to "audit" did not meet with success; I soon found out that Hubbard's claim and my wishful thinking were both inaccurate. It seemed difficult for her to grasp the fundamentals; she would hesitate to put her patient into certain incidents and would often elicit more annoyance than therapeutic benefits. After several unsuccessful attempts to become a dianetic practitioner she rebelled at continuing, and I made no effort to dissuade her.

In April, 1950 the Hubbard Dianetic Research Foundation was incorporated; the expressed purpose was to disseminate knowledge of this new system of psychotherapy, continuing the process which was to begin with the book

Dianetics. It was planned—or perhaps I should say hoped—to stimulate interest in further research by independent investigators, with the Foundation acting as a clearing-house of information. The Foundation would engage in commercial activities only so far as necessary to keep up with current expenses; any profits or endowments would be spent for further research carried on or subsidized by the Foundation.

When it was suggested that I be assigned the duties of medical director, I accepted without qualms, as I could foresee an opportunity for continuing with my investigations of the human mind. I realized that some of my more captious brethren might criticize my acceptance of such a position, but I felt that the contributions to knowledge which would ensue would ultimately counteract any criticism.

One of the first official duties of the Foundation was to present the concepts of dianetics to a group of psychiatrists, educators and lay people in Washington, D.C. Some of the psychiatrists—perhaps the more progressive and open-minded ones—had evinced an interest in the novel postulates and intriguing conclusions of dianetics. Hubbard's book had been on the stands for about a month, and was already a topic for discussion in psychiatric circles.

I did not feel that the Washington venture was a successful one—at least, not from the medical point of view. It was noteworthy that most of the people whose interest in dianetics had been augmented by this presentation were members of the laity, rather than the profession, and I thought that I could detect in their attitudes the fervor of the convert, rather than the cool, objective interest of the scientist. The professional people evidenced an interest in the philosophy of dianetics; their interest was repelled, however, by the manner of presentation of the subject, especially the unwarranted implication that it was necessary to repudiate one's previous beliefs before accepting dianetics.

We returned to New Jersey around the first of June and plunged into a maelstrom of activity. There was a tremendous flood of correspondence to be answered, and the demand for training in the technique of "auditing" was overwhelming. Applicants for training were accepted as they applied, without investigation as to their qualifications or motives. On several occasions I expressed my perturbation at this policy, but my objections were overridden by the majority of the Board of Trustees.

It soon became apparent that neither my medical knowledge nor my past experience in research was going to be utilized. I found, rather, that my time was spent in administrative work, in teaching and in giving demonstrations. I saw a few patients, but seldom had the opportunity to follow them through; a few sessions and the patient had to be turned over to one of the students for the continuation of his therapy.

It was a period of intense confusion and rapid expansion, with little or no opportunity for analysis of accomplishments or for consideration of future developments. In spite of this, I found my appraisal of dianetics becoming more and more clear.

There were several elements which seemed to be of importance: the cardinal point was that there was a difference between the ideals inherent within the dianetic hypothesis and the actions of the Foundation in its ostensible efforts to carry out these ideals. The ideals of dianetics, as I saw them, included non-authoritarianism and a flexibility of approach; they did not exclude the realization that this hypothesis might not be absolutely perfect. The ideals of dianetics continued to be given lip-service, but I could see a definite disparity between ideals and actualities.

Other points in my appraisal which I thought important were the evidences of potential dangers in the method, the inability to confirm Hubbard's concept of "clear" and the effects of positive suggestion.

In my early investigation of dianetics, I had seen no evidence of danger in dianetic therapy. After Hubbard's book was published, however, and people less well-grounded in the precepts of psychotherapy began "auditing," it became apparent that dianetics was not entirely innocuous. It was called to my attention that two individuals had developed acute psychoses subsequent to dianetic "processing." Both of these people had apparently been sane prior to this time; they were neurotic and unhappy, but yet adapted to society sufficiently well so that their conduct fell within the bounds of social acceptability. One, a woman, developed an acute manic psychosis, characterized by the usual increased psychomotor activity, disorientation, delusions and deterioration. It became necessary to institutionalize her, as any further attempts at dianetic therapy were ineffectual.

The second patient, a man, sought dianetics in an attempt to secure relief from a peptic ulcer. A week of therapy saw alleviation of his ulcer symptoms, but he too became manic. He disappeared from the Foundation for a few days; when he returned, he had with him a man whom he introduced as "one of my disciples, St. Simon." With further dianetic therapy there was a decrease in his manic symptoms, and shortly thereafter he discontinued treatment.

In both these cases it is possible that there was a history of prior psychotic episodes; moreover, I have no information as to any modification in the technique of therapy used, as these individuals did not come to my attention until after the psychosis developed. In the confusion consequent upon the sudden great popular interest in dianetics it was impossible for me to observe every case; further, it had already developed that the policy of the Foundation was not to be one of any particular discrimination in the selection or management of cases.

These unhappy incidents were the first major exception to the dianetic hypothesis which I had seen, and I was deeply concerned. The precipitation of psychosis by psychotherapy is highly important, and I did not wish to dismiss this occurrence as a regrettable and unforeseen accident. It is well known that any sort of manipulation of the mind can eventuate in profound mental disturbance; psychoanalysis, narcosynthesis and hypnosis had been followed by psychotic "breaks" long before dianetics appeared on the scene.

Nor did I feel that it would be sufficient for me to issue a warning that dianetics was dangerous and should be avoided. I felt, rather, that these occurrences were a challenge to clearer thinking and more operational explanation.

When one is confronted with an exception to a hypothesis which he is using, there are two ways in which the exception can be accounted for. One, it can be explained in terms of the hypothesis; secondly, the hypothesis can be re-examined and modified in such a way as to account for the exception. Using the dianetic frame of reference, it might be easy to explain why these patients had become psychotic. One could say that they had numerous engram-commands, some of which could produce a manic effect, others whose activation would result in depression. Dianetics had removed a sufficient number of the depressive engrams and re-activated enough of the manic engrams to produce a psychosis.

The dianetic explanation for the precipitation of a psychosis does not satisfy me completely; I find that the conventional explanations are equally dissatisfying. For example, it might be said that a neurotic patient, when he approaches a "danger area" in therapy, marshals his defenses to resist the encroachment of the therapeutic probing. With the mobilization of defenses go such states as fear, anger or anxiety; should these increase, psychosis results.

To me this seems to be a description of successive occurrences, rather than an explanation. I find that I can maintain a more dynamic approach to such problems if I ask such questions as, "Why does a person act as if he prefers psychosis to sanity? What experiences has he had which make him act as if he has only these two alternatives? What would happen if he didn't become psychotic? What would happen— or better, what does he think would happen—if he remained sane?"

It is most unfortunate that these patients, in their efforts to secure a promised greater sanity, appeared to lose what sanity they had. Yet a larger benefit may accrue as a result of this observation: if we can find out how a psychosis is precipitated, we are that much closer to discovering how to cure it.

Among the promising factors which mitigate these unfortunate occurrences are the reports that there have been several cases in which patients have ceased to be psychotic following dianetic therapy. I have observed only one of these cases, and that superficially; I am, therefore, not in a position to say that this is a proof of the efficacy of dianetics. It makes me believe, however, that further investigation with proper controls may furnish us with useful information.

Another point in which dianetics did not seem to follow out the claims of its originator was in the concept of "clear." Hubbard defines a "clear" as an individual who, through dianetic therapy, has had all his engrams removed, who "has neither active nor potential psychosomatic illness or aberration" (p. 170). He further states that an engram, once removed, is gone permanently, and can never return to influence a person's behavior. In our early correspondence he mentioned that a "clear" had been obtained in as few as twenty hours of therapy; this sort of result has not, to my knowledge, been obtained by other practitioners of dianetics. I know of persons who have had 1500 to 2000 hours of therapy and do not approximate the state of "clear," as defined. True, they are in better health and are more effectual and happy citizens —but they have not reached this absolute goal.

I have yet to see a "clear" before and after dianetic therapy. I have not reached that state myself, nor have I been able to produce that state in any of my patients. I have seen some individuals who are supposed to be "clear," but their behavior does not conform to the definition of the state. Moreover, an individual supposed to have been "clear" has undergone a relapse into conduct which suggests an incipient psychosis.

This does *not* mean that I am denying the existence of the state of being "clear." It remains a theoretical possibility, granting the validity of certain postulates. I must, however, regard this claim as one which has not been confirmed.

The state of "clear," according to Hubbard, depends on the phenomenon called "erasure," which consists in the disappearance of all pain and all perceptic content from an engram which has been recounted a sufficient number of times. The disappearance is supposed to be total and permanent, and the information contained in the event is said to be filed elsewhere in the memory banks, where it is no longer capable of aberrating the patient's behavior.

I have observed the phenomenon numerous times; the patient reaches a point in recounting an engram where he will laugh and say, "Isn't that silly? I just can't remember what I was saying." Both people who have been students of dianetics and those who know nothing about the subject whatsoever have

demonstrated this behavior. When these incidents are looked
for again, however, after a lapse of a few days, they have been
noted sometimes to recur with as much discomfort as was previously experienced. My associates confirm this observation.

The explanation of this according to the dianetic theory is
that the complete content of the incident has not been recovered; the patient may not have sonic recall, or there may be
some painful emotion connected with the incident which has
not been reduced, or there may be an earlier similar event. I
feel, however, that there is another explanation which requires
a modification of the dianetic theory. This concept will be discussed later in greater detail.

Another observation which I made during my association
with the Foundation had to do with the phenomenon called
"positive suggestion." It has been known since the days of the
Egyptians that most people can be put into a state in which
they act as if whatever they are told is true; they are said to
be hypnotized, and the statements made by the operator in
manipulating the subject's actions are called "positive suggestions." Hubbard in his book had inveighed against hypnosis and pointed out that being hypnotized was tantamount to
being given an engram.

It has been known for some time that hypnosis can alter a
person's behavior pattern for better or worse, not only during
the hypnotic state but also for an indefinite period thereafter.*
It was generally believed, however, that the person had to be
in the hypnotic state in order to have a positive suggestion
installed and his conduct thereby altered.

During my first acquaintance with dianetics I had supposed
that it was a form of hypnosis; patients in "reverie" manifested all the signs of the hypnoidal state as defined by Davis

*Werner Wolff, *The Threshold of the Abnormal*, Hermitage House, Inc., New
York, 1950, p. 328.

and Husband.* When I discussed this with Hubbard, he pointed out numerous reasons why, in his opinion, dianetics was different from hypnosis. I remained unconvinced of their complete dissimilarity and frequently found myself in agreement with critics who pointed out their parallel manifestations.

One observation in particular enabled me, I feel, to relate dianetics and hypnosis in an operational manner. According to the Hubbardian hypothesis, all aberrated conduct stems from the engram, an event characterized by unconsciousness and pain, which might result from physical trauma, anesthesia, electric shock, "painful emotion" or hypnosis. Further, the existence of an engram could be verified by the behavior of a patient during his recollection of the event; if the patient yawned, stretched, underwent a mood-change ("a rise in tone-level") and acted as if he had re-evaluated the event, the event was an engram by definition.

I began to notice that some experiences produced engram-like effects when reviewed, although the events did *not* contain trauma, anesthesia, etc. Statements which Hubbard had made to me in ordinary conversation, statements which I had made to the students, statements made to patients when they were fully conscious and comfortable were, when subjected to dianetic recall, observed to produce a similar response to that seen in a "valid" engram. Not all statements produced this effect, however; the engram-like response was seen when the statements tended to restrict a person's choice of action or his ability to differentiate.

In other words, it seemed as if a person could be hypnotized by ordinary conversation; ordinary informational statements could, under some circumstances, have the same effects as a

*Davis, L. W. and Husband, R. W., "A Study of Hypnotic Susceptibility in Relation to Personality Traits," *J. Abnorm. and Soc. Psychol.*, 26:175; 1931.

hypnotic positive suggestion, even when the recipient of the information was wide awake.

I found, moreover, that each person acted as if he had an orderly list of those from whom he would accept positive suggestion with varying degrees of willingness. In general, those who headed such lists were parents and loved ones; a simple statement coming from one of these had the force of a command. Next in the hierarchy came teachers, doctors and those in positions of authority, while at the bottom of the list were those who had made demonstrably false statements and those who had caused pain; statements made by the latter persons were ignored or negated against. It is, of course, possible for a person to occupy two positions on this list: the doctor or parent might cause pain, or the loved one might be detected in a lie. I suggest that this may be a factor in the developing of ambivalence or mixed feelings toward certain people.

In general, however, I found that I, as a doctor, could make positive suggestions which would alter a person's conduct much more easily than could a person whose position in society was less respected. The implications of this have done much to make me aware of my responsibilities to the people with whom I speak.

As a corollary of these observations I found that the simplest restrictive statements, even when the listener was fully conscious, tended to alter responses. For example, I have tried to recall a conversation with a colleague and found myself unable to remember what he said; when I recollected that during the course of the conversation he had said, "I don't remember," then I was able to recall the remainder of his words. It apparently makes no difference as to what pronoun is used; "I don't remember" and "You don't remember" seem to have an equally restrictive effect on the listener. The restrictive effect occurred; when I became aware that there was a restriction of my action of remembering, I was no longer restricted.

I have also found that therapeutic benefits could be obtained by utilizing the converse of this mechanism. During therapy I use a great number of *permissive* positive suggestions: "You *can* remember; you *may* obey this command or not, as you wish; you *can* understand this; you *do* know; you *can* differentiate." Compare, if you will, these phrases and their potential effects with the *restrictive* positive suggestions, such as "You can't; you mustn't; you're stupid."

The idea of the permissive positive suggestion is admittedly simple; it is so simple that it is frequently overlooked. A recent example indicating the effectuality of permissive suggestion comes to mind: on a visit to an obstetrical ward I observed one of the residents trying to examine a psychotic woman who was in labor. He met with considerable resistance on her part, which led him to say, "Now, look at the way you're moving around! You've got your hands right there so I can't do a thing! You're not helping me—you're just making things worse!"

After a struggle, the resident succeeded in completing the examination and left the room. One of the medical students remarked that he would like to examine the patient also, but didn't relish the idea of precipitating another battle, so I offered my assistance. I spoke to the woman, saying, "You can let the doctor examine you. This does not have to disturb you. You can lie still, if you want to. You can keep your hands on your chest." The student was then able to examine the patient without the slightest difficulty.

I have seen a similar effect obtained with the use of permissive suggestion in a markedly inaccessible catatonic, a man who had been practically mute for over ten years. Constant, quiet repetition of the permissive phrase, "You can talk, if you want to. You don't have to stay quiet," has elicited some lucid conversation.

With these observations I feel that I have become better aware of the relationship between dianetics and hypnosis. They are both forms of communication, each seeking to change a person's behavior. In hypnosis the subject is influenced to conform to the will, the choices or the whims of the operator; in dianetics we try to enable the patient to make the best choice possible to him. By using permissive, rather than restrictive, suggestions we aim at making available the full range of a person's potentialities.

During the time I was making these observations I was continuing with my work for the Foundation. I spent some time in California, and directed the opening of the Chicago branch. I observed improvements in patients with Buerger's disease, with epilepsy, with allergies. I saw two patients with neoplasms, who did not deteriorate as rapidly as prognosticated. In general, there was nothing that I observed in dianetic therapy—even as it was practiced at that time—which could lead me to change my opinion that the dianetic technique furnished one of the most useful and promising tools yet placed in medical hands. I was aware of its shortcomings, but these only served as a challenge for further study.

By October, 1950, I had come to the conclusion that I could not agree with all the tenets of dianetics as set forth by the Foundation. I could not, as previously mentioned, support Hubbard's claims regarding the state of "clear." I no longer felt, as I once had, that any intelligent person could (and presumably should) practice dianetics. I noted several points on which the actions of the Foundation were at variance with the expressed ideals of dianetics: one of these points was a tendency toward the development of an authoritarian attitude. Moreover, there was a poorly concealed attitude of disparagement of the medical profession and of the efforts of previous workers in the field of mental illness. Finally, the avowed purpose of the Foundation—the accomplishment of precise scientific research into the functioning of the mind—was conspicuously absent.

I expressed my opinion on these matters to the Board of Trustees on several occasions, with no discernible effect. Nor was I alone in my disagreement with Foundation policies; those of us who advocated a more conservative attitude were in the minority, however, and our efforts were unavailing. I, therefore, felt it incumbent upon me to submit my resignation.

I felt at that time—and I am still thoroughly convinced—that the practice of this or any other form of psychotherapy requires an indoctrination which could not be accomplished by the Foundation. To be a good psychotherapist one should have more than a superficial knowledge of the functioning of the human body, should have more than average experience in the various ways in which human beings behave, and should be imbued with ethical considerations for the welfare of others. True, a lay psychotherapist can practice his art with benefit to his patients—but there is a niche in the practice of psychotherapy which can be filled only by one who has had medical training.

I feel also that medical practice might be improved by utilization of some of the observations which have been noted in dianetics. However, in order to make any new idea acceptable to the medical profession, it should be presented in a scientific manner. That, I fear, is not going to happen so long as the Foundation pursues its present policies.

Because of the nature of the publicity which the Foundation has received in various newspapers and magazines, there has been considerable confusion and alarm in some circles. While this is understandable, a great deal of this confusion has resulted from the failure to differentiate between the hypothesis and technique of dianetics and the application of that technique by the Foundation. Moreover, one must also differentiate between dianetics, the hypothesis, and *Dianetics,* the book by L. Ron Hubbard. If one is careful to make such differentiations, it becomes obvious that there is nothing alarming about the dianetic hypothesis *per se;* at worst, it can only be inaccurate—and my investigations definitely do *not* lead me to that conclusion.

Insofar as the dangers of dianetic therapy are concerned, they are no greater than those inherent in many other therapies; in my opinion, the effectiveness of dianetics far outweighs its possible dangers. However, there is one danger which lurks in *all* forms of healing, no matter whether the efforts are directed at the psyche or the soma: we should beware of overenthusiasm, especially when the enthusiast is unskilled and uncritical. If one regards any hypothesis as a perfect, closed system, one which gives an invariably correct answer to every question, he is asking for trouble. A persistent scientific scepticism and an ethical regard for the rights of one's patients must be maintained in the practice of dianetics as it should be in any other form of therapy; in the absence of that attitude any therapeutic method is apt to be dangerous.

Perhaps at this point it would be permissible for me to state again that I regard the hypothesis of dianetics and certain aspects of the technique as immensely important. It is admittedly similar in numerous respects to other hypotheses of mental function; yet there are differences which make it much more operational than any other hypotheses known to me at this time. It is possible, using the dianetic viewpoint, to re-examine the work of psychiatric pioneers and discover more meaningfulness in their observations; we can also make more cogent explanations for the successes and failures of previous psycho-therapies. We can even note where Hubbardian dianetics has departed from dianetic tenets, with adverse results.

Most important of all, dianetics seems to give us a new answer to some of the questions we ask about human behavior. I do not say that it gives us *the* answer: whether it does or not must await years of testing and observation. But it gives us a fresh viewpoint and a new *modus operandi*, both of which have been badly needed. In order for Mankind to progress, it is necessary for answers to be given, for answers are action. Even a wrong answer is closer to the truth than an apathetic "I don't know"; a wrong answer can be proved to be wrong, and the correct answer sought, while unquestioning ignorance or hopelessness leads only to stagnation.

———— II ————

Hᴜʙʙᴀʀᴅ ꜱᴛᴀᴛᴇꜱ in his book *Dianetics* that Man is motivated solely by the will to survive. His survival activities operate through four different drives, called "dynamics": the first is survival of the individual, the second the survival of his mate and his progeny, the third the survival of his group and the fourth the survival of all Mankind. All of Man's activities have a survival value, and each activity can be located somewhere on the spectrum of the dynamics.

The integrating factor of all survival activities is the function of the mind. The body is the structure which survives; the mind is the function of that structure. Included in the dianetic concept of the mind is the entire gamut of survival activities, from respiration, digestion and excretion up to creative imagination, calculation and prediction.

It is as if the mind works on two levels, the analytic and the reactive. The analytic mind has to do with perceptions of differences, with abstractions and with the synthesis of old concepts into new mental artifacts. The function of consciousness (or "awareness") is limited to the analytic portion of the mind; when a person is unconscious, his analytic mind is not functioning and vice versa.

The reactive mind, on the other hand, never ceases to function. It is constantly registering perceptions. The perceptions are stored as if they were recordings; they are not meaningful in a human sense until and unless they are subjected to the scrutiny of the analytic mind. The sole aim of the reactive mind, according to Hubbard, is biological survival.

Certain events as perceived by the reactive mind have an extremely high survival value. The events, called "engrams," occur during a time when the organism is subjected to pain and unconsciousness (also called "anaten" or attenuation of analytic mind function). The perceptual data contained in engrams appear to have a command value; they say, in essence, "Here is an occurrence wherein death was threatened, but you survived. The next time such a situation presents itself, do exactly as you did the first time, and you will again survive. You must, moreover, act according to the verbal content of the engram."

There is a further step in the functioning of the engram. In order to insure that the engram-command is obeyed, it is as if the pain in it were used to enforce the command. The engram-command also says, "If you don't do exactly as was done the first time, or if you don't do what the engram says, you are going to suffer the pain you did when the engram was installed."

To give an example of this, let us suppose that a man gets into an altercation in a tavern where there is a strong odor of beer; he receives a blow on the head and is rendered momentarily unconscious. During his period of unconsciousness someone says, "You're no good! Get out of here!"

We have here all the elements of an engram; the pain in the head resulting from the blow; the unconsciousness; the perceptic content of odor and words. A mental circuit has been established, and it lies dormant waiting to be reactivated.

Now let us suppose that this man goes to a party at a friend's house a few weeks after his injury. There is a smell of beer in the air—a smell which, as a result of his engram, is associated with pain and therefore means "Danger!" Suppose someone says jokingly, "You're no good." There will be a strong tendency for our man to leave the party and go somewhere else; the engram-command says, "Get out of here!" If he is persuaded to remain, he is apt to develop a headache, which will further augment his urge to "get out of here." If he leaves, he will probably notice that the headache disappears quite rapidly.

Other possibilities may occur. If someone says, "Get out of here," the man must admit that he is "no good"; if he doesn't, the headache is apt to occur. Or if he should develop a headache, he feels as if he must say that he is "no good," and he must also "get out of here." But "here" is not a specific location; wherever he is is "here." This engram-command cannot be obeyed, so the headache is apt to persist until some other event occurs which can temporarily inactivate the circuit.

This is the method of reacting to an engram-command, as postulated by dianetics. A man might react in such a manner if he had only one engram. It is highly improbable, however, that anyone would have only one of these stimulus-response patterns; he would be more likely to have a vast number of them, and the integrated total would make up his field of aberration—or, according to dianetics, the content of his reactive mind.

It is a characteristic of the reactive mind that it is unable to perceive differences; one time is identical with every other time, one percept within the engram is identical with every other percept in that engram. Reactions of the reactive mind, therefore, are stereotyped and illogical in that they are not necessarily congruent with nor appropriate to the situation presented.

The aim of dianetic therapy is to subject these illogical relationships to review by the analytical mind. By so doing, the patient obtains insight into his reactions and is able to choose the best reaction pattern for a given stimulus pattern.

But insight is not the only effect obtained by dianetics. It has been found that the pain which was experienced as part of the engram is also stored as a "memory." This "remembered" pain—in dianetic terminology called a "somatic"—can be brought up to the level of perception by repeating the words in the engramic situation. Moreover, by continued repetition of the words, and reviewing the perception of this painful period, the "somatic" disappears. Whether this erasure of a pain memory is permanent or not is a matter for further investigation; it is one of the claims of dianetics that such an erasure results in complete and permanent disappearance.

It also seems as if the command-effect of an engram is enforced by the existence of the somatic. When the somatic is erased, the engram loses its command value, and the patient is no longer constrained to make a stereotyped response to a given stimulus-pattern.

In order to achieve these therapeutic aims, the patient is assisted to a state known as "reverie." Reverie seems to be similar to the "hypnoidal state" and is characterized by relaxation and a fine fluttering of the closed eyelids. In this state there is a certain amount of attenuation of analytical mind function, which seems to permit the stored "memories" of the reactive mind to enter the zone of awareness. During this state, as distinguished to some degree from the hypnotic, the patient appears to be in full control of himself, can make choices and decisions freely and is not receptive to the type of positive suggestions wherein his mind is controlled by the will of another.

Once a patient is in reverie, he brings up with the assistance of the auditor the problems which concern him, whether they be primarily psychic or somatic or both. The auditor (so called because his function is that of listening to the patient) assists the patient to review completely the situations in which a certain pattern of conduct was learned. When any of these situations are found to be painful, the patient is encouraged to bring up the "memory" of the pain and review the situation until the pain is reduced or erased. Then a search for an earlier situation is made, until the patient feels that he has reached and examined the initial engram of this particular reaction-pattern.

It is found that the majority of patients act as if some of the early painful engrams were acquired during the intra-uterine period. It is interesting to observe that therapeutic results can be obtained even if the patient does not believe in the possibility of prenatal "memory." The *actual* existence of prenatal memory is, in my opinion, of secondary importance; of primary importance is the observation that the patient seems to benefit from reviewing such "memories" and from having the concomitant pain reduced.

Classical dianetic theory states that the earliest engram must be reviewed and erased if one is to obtain permanent benefit; my own experience is that, in general, the earlier the engram which is reviewed, the greater the therapeutic benefits obtained.

When the patient is in the state of reverie, it is assumed that everything he says is part of, or relevant to, the content of an engram. It is also assumed that he is making the responses which have been requested of him. If the patient is asked to "go to the earliest moment of pain which is available" and if he says, "I don't feel anything," it is assumed that the patient is in an engram which has as part of its content the words, "I don't feel anything." If the patient should say, "I don't know what you want me to do," it is assumed that the words, "I don't know," are in the engram, and so on.

The auditor attempts to direct the patient's attention to a specific moment of discomfort, the earliest one which the patient can recall. He asks the patient to recall and re-experience everything which occurred at that time, and also to feel the discomfort which accompanies the event. The patient is required to recount and re-recount the scene until the associated discomfort has disappeared.

At this juncture, let me call your attention to an experiment which can be performed to illustrate the dianetic technique. Take a person who has recently incurred some trivial injury —say, a burn from a cigarette or a bump on the head. Tell the person to close his eyes and "go back" * to the time he hurt himself. Say to him, "Notice what you're doing at the instant you get hurt. What do you see? What do you hear? What background noises are there? What odors are in the air? Try to feel the position of your body. Try to feel the pain. Notice how you feel, what your mood is at this particular instant. Now, go through this experience again and tell me what you get. Feel the pain. Notice the sights, the sounds, etc."

In such a fashion, have the person review the painful incident at least eight or ten times. In the majority of instances, the patient will report that the pain becomes more intense at the second or third recounting, then diminishes rapidly until it disappears entirely. Moreover, it is a clinical

---

* (This phrase seldom requires any explanation to the patient; it seems to be readily understood as a suggestion to re-experience rather than to "remember.")

impression that injuries so treated heal much more rapidly than is usual. It also seems that it is necessary to review *all* the content of this segment of time; if the patient overlooks or omits a portion of the experience, the relief from the pain is not so complete.

As an example of this, some months ago I slipped while getting out of the car and fell, landing on my outstretched hands. The strain on my wrists was considerable, and there was definite discomfort in them. At my first opportunity I attempted to recount this incident to myself, directing my attention to all aspects of my sensorium. About ten recountings of the event and the pain in my wrists diminished, although not so much as I had expected. About four hours later, I became aware of a pain in my right knee. I reviewed the event of my injury again, including the injury to the knee, which I had apparently overlooked in the first recountings. The pain in both the wrists and the knee promptly disappeared and did not recur.

This technique is the essence of dianetics. It includes looking for a *specific* event of injury, of directing one's awareness to all concepts which were acquired during that segment of time, and of repeating the re-examination of the event until the pain content is exhausted.

It is in this technique that the major differences between dianetics and the older psychotherapies lie; specificity of event, totality of content and repetition to exhaustion are not, to my knowledge, included in any other method of treating psychic or psychosomatic illness.

It is applicable to events of somatic trauma, where there is an observable injury, and to events of psychic trauma, where the injured one acts as if in pain without having observable injury. A person may have had an experience which makes him "feel badly"—a disappointment, a disagreement, a quarrel; having him recount the event fully will produce similar results. He will no longer "feel badly," and he is much less apt to bear ill-will or resentment toward the person who may have caused the traumatic experience. The event, after dianetic recounting, seems to be evaluated objectively, with less emotional coloring.

There is another concept in dianetics which is, I believe, a highly operational one. This is the concept of *valence*.

Valence may be defined as the role which a person plays in response to certain stimulus patterns. It is postulated that this role was learned at a time of pain and/or unconsciousness, and that the role has a higher survival value than the one which the patient had been constrained to play.

For example, a child is ill or injured. The doctor helps to alleviate the discomfort. The doctor has a cough. In the future, then, whenever the patient tries to alleviate the discomfort of another, he coughs. He plays the role of the doctor, and part of that role is the cough. Coughing is a symbol of the doctor's valence.

Coughing may represent numerous other things besides this, but one of the meanings of cough to this patient is, "I am helping someone else."

Instead of the cough, the patient may adopt any of numerous other attributes; he may, in assuming another's valence, use the other's phraseology, or he may act as the other person states. Suppose that the doctor had said, "I'm tired." The patient, when playing the role of a doctor, would either tend to say, "I'm tired," or he would be tired. It would seem to make no difference what the doctor meant by "tired"; he might have meant that he was fatigued or he might have meant that he was "tired" (i.e. resentful) of paying taxes. No matter what the doctor meant, the patient in assuming the doctor's valence seems to interpret the words literally and to react in that fashion.

Taking on the valence of another has a survival value. Certainly, if there is illness, it is better to be the doctor than the patient. But one does not, in actuality, recover from an illness by acting as does a doctor. He recovers by the mobilization and utilization of his own powers of resistance, and so it appears as if the patient is hindering his own recovery by his non-analytical attempts to be someone else. The survival value of a valence seems to be a specious one.

The concept of valence and the phenomenon which can be described as being out of one's own valence and/or in some other person's valence is useful in reaching a better understanding of mental disorders. Take the homosexual, for example: the male homosexual might be said to be a male who is in a feminine valence. In the sex act, there is a higher survival value in being a woman—so his reactive mind tells him. He may hate himself for acting like a woman, but he does so, nevertheless. It can be seen, moreover, that he is acting like a *specific* female in his own past experience; by finding the female whose valence he has assumed we can help to rid him of his neurosis.

It also appears as if a person can shift into his own valence of an earlier time. The adult who sulks and pouts can be said to have assumed the valence of himself as a child. The catatonic who lies in the foetal position, who requires nourishment by tube, may have reverted to his own prenatal valence, if one chooses to believe that this is possible.

In therapy we should be aware of the situations and command-statements which might act as valence shifters. The patient should be assisted to the realization that the assumption of another's valence is not necessarily the behavior which has the highest survival value.

The foregoing represents an attempt at a synopsis of Hubbard's hypothesis as expressed in his book. Those who have read his work will note that I have omitted some of the concepts he uses, such as the "file clerk," the "somatic strip" and "demon circuits."

It is my opinion that the use of anthropomorphic analogies is apt to lead to semantic confusion. Perhaps there is a function of the mind similar to that of a file-clerk, but it would seem less confusing if that function were described rather than designated, even figuratively, as a human form complete with green eye-shade.

It has been observed, moreover, that one should be cautious in using anthropomorphisms in scientific works. The statement that the mind works like a calculating machine contains a modicum of truth—but it is one of those statements which is often misinterpreted to mean that the mind works *only* like a calculating machine, which is an obvious absurdity. The human mind is a complex affair—not too complex, perhaps, for us to understand it, but not so simple that we can accurately say that it works "just like" anything else. The human mind works just like the human mind, and I am not willing to detract from its uniqueness by over-simplified mechanistic devices. Moreover, it may be pointed out that a calculating machine works like the human mind because it was invented by the human mind.

MODIFICATIONS OF A
HYPOTHESIS OF MENTAL
FUNCTION

———— III ————

Let us define the mind as the integrated totality of all functions of the organism. Its functioning seems to work on three different levels: perception of the environment (both external and internal), storage of perceptual data and re-assembly of data. These functions, in turn, seem to work on an off-on system of awareness of difference; used in this sense, awareness is equivalent to the ability to react. In other words, if an organism reacts to a change of light, it can be said to be "aware" of a change; the organism differentiates between one amount of light and another.

All perceptions may be considered on the basis of differentiation. Seeing a piece of paper consists in differentiating between color of paper and color of not-paper, between shape of paper and shape of not-paper, between feel of paper and feel of not-paper, etc.

It seems as if living organisms can choose between reacting and not-reacting, the choice being made on the basis of past experience. We choose to make reactions which, in the past, have led away from pain and the threat of death, preferring reactions which lead towards continuing action.

The process of living, then, may be said to be a continuous process of receiving informational data from all parts of the sensorium, comparing this data with data previously registered, choosing a course of action which seems to have the highest survival value, and acting on the basis of that choice. Let us call these processes "feeling" (physical sensation), "remembering," "thinking" and "acting," respectively.

Consider the "thinking" process of a one-celled organism which is floating in an aqueous substrate. It can react to changes in its environment—or, to express it another way, some changes in its environment will cause observable changes in the functioning of the cell. The external changes which might alter cellular functions are changes in pressure, in temperature, in the chemical environment, in light and in the electrical field which surrounds the cell. Pressure can vary in the area which affects the cell; the pressure change may affect the entire cell, as when the barometric pressure varies; it may affect part of the cell, as when the cell is rotated with a consequent alteration in centrifugal force; pressure can also be applied intermittently, different frequencies producing different responses. One part of the spectrum of intermittently varying pressure is called "sound."

Observation of the behavior of one-celled organisms also suggests that it is possible to postulate a sort of cellular "memory." I suspect that training—and on this level of abstraction "training," "learning" and "memory" are practically synonymous—occurs because there has been an alteration in the structure and function of the protoplasm of the cell. In this I am in agreement with von Foerster and his concept of "punched protein molecules" as the units of memory.

"Cellular memory"—or, better, protoplasmic memory might be defined as the state which exists in a cell after it has been exposed to a force sufficient to alter the spatial configuration of the protein molecules. A force is exerted on the cell which, in essence, crystallizes the protein in such a manner that it will no longer react to another presentation of a similar force. It is obvious that the function of "memory" implies a difference in reaction to successive applications of similar stimuli; I suggest that the difference occurs as a result of the change created by the first experience.

This theorizing would hardly be germane to the discussion if it were not necessary to stipulate that we seem to have *two* types of "memory." The first type, which I suggest is on a cellular or protoplasmic level, is the memory of data—the phenomenon which makes it possible for us to know that we have had past experience which is recognizable. In the future, we shall refer to this as "perception-registration."

The other sort of "memory," the one with which we deal primarily in therapy, is that which results from associations among data. This is the sort of memory which causes us to associate red with danger, loud noises with pain, or beauty with pleasure. In contradistinction to "cellular memory," which seems to be relatively permanent, this associative memory is quite ephemeral and labile, changing and capable of change. It seems that associative memory is a function of the central nervous system, of the specialized neuronal cells, rather than a function of undifferentiated cellular elements.

But to return to the discussion of "memory" as a general cellular function: if a cell is capable of responding to a force, we might say that it is *aware* of the force; its ability to respond might also be spoken of as cellular consciousness. Conversely, when it cannot or does not respond to a force, we might say that it is not aware or is unconscious. Some cells, especially those in the central nervous system, can respond characteristically to an appropriate stimulus; if the stimulus is presented again, after a certain interval the cell will respond again in its characteristic manner. During that certain interval, however, the cell is incapable of responding to the stimulus; this interval is known as the "refractory period." I suggest that this may also be called cellular unconsciousness.

Supposing that we have an aggregation of cells and a force is applied to one of them. It has been shown that there is a piezo-electric effect in certain proteins: application of pressure to protein substances can generate a minute electric current or can produce a change in the electrical field. If one cell is subjected to a force and it generates a current, that current will affect the neighboring cell, which will in turn affect its neighbor and so on. The application of a force to a cell might also cause a difference in the excretory products of the cell; these would produce a change in the chemical substrate of the next cell, and so on.

Let us assume that there are two types of cells in this aggregation, one which had most to do with nutrition, the other having most to do with locomotion. Suppose that the nutrition cells were subjected to a noxious stimulus which prevented them from functioning. It would seem to be of definite survival value if the "unconsciousness" of the nutrition cells were to be an appropriate stimulus for increased function of the locomotion cells, especially if the function were directed away from the region of the noxious stimulus. It is safe to say that an organism which did not behave in this manner would not survive for long.

We have here an example of a simple, primitive organism which reacts according to its innate capabilities in a manner which helps it to survive. It may be that the human mind works on a basis as simple as this, achieving its complexity with the combination of large numbers of simple units of function. In other words, we might suggest an atomistic theory of mental function, with the constituent atoms being the "mind" of each individual cell.

The most important function of the mind, whether protozoan or metazoan, seems to be differentiation. In the human mind the function of differentiation seems to be represented by a hierarchy of complexity. For example, there is a neuromuscular mechanism connected with the pupil of the eye, which regulates the aperture of the pupil; when light increases, the pupil constricts, and when the light decreases in intensity, the pupil dilates in order to permit more light to fall on the retina. We can say that this reflex is "conscious" so long as it continues to function. When a person is subjected to anesthesia, there is a stage when this reflex no longer obtains; the pupil dilates and no amount of light will make it constrict. I suggest that this can be called the stage of pupillary unconsciousness.

On a higher level of function we might take a man who has had numerous experiences with brunette women and, as a result, he no longer responds to brunettes in the same way that he responds to non-brunettes. We might say that he has reached the level of brunette unconsciousness.

The criterion of unconsciousness seems to be the ability to differentiate, to react to two different stimuli in two different ways. If the pupil reacts to light in the same manner as it does to no-light, it is unconscious; if the man responds to brunette Alice in the same way he responds to brunette Mary, he is, in a sense, unconscious—he does not differentiate between brunettes.

The ability to differentiate implies that we must have a recording of past experiences which can be referred to for comparison with present experiences. I suspect, on the basis of observations made, that there is a *constant and continuous* recording process of all stimuli which impinge on one's sensorium. I cannot say with accuracy how long these recordings are available for recall and review, but it seems that their period of availability is much longer than is suspected in contemporary psychology.

Nor can I say with accuracy when this recording process begins. My patients act as if they had recordings of what went on at their births, and they frequently act as if they were recording impressions of their prenatal existence. At the present stage of investigation, I can see no reason for *not* postulating that an embryo can record perceptions; there are, in fact, many cogent reasons for postulating that some type of prenatal "memory" is an innate function of the human mind. I have been informed that investigative work with results confirming this postulate is now being pursued and is near completion.

These somewhat random preliminary remarks having been made, it is now feasible to discuss the hypothesis of mental function which is presently being used by our group as a basis for the practice of psychotherapy. This hypothesis is a modification of the one presented by Hubbard, and appears to be more operational and productive of greater therapeutic benefits for our patients. The modifications were made as a result of numerous discussions with many different people; it would therefore be inaccurate for me to say that they are mine and mine alone. Suffice it to say that all of us who are interested in psychotherapy have contributed to the improvements; mine is the task of the amanuensis, rather than the honor of the innovator.

One concept contained in the hypothesis which is at present in use by our group can be expressed graphically (see Fig. 1).

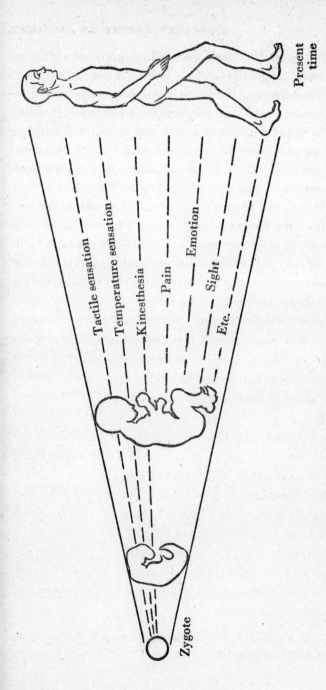

Present time

Tactile sensation
Temperature sensation
Kinesthesia
Pain
Emotion
Sight
Etc.

Zygote

Fig. 1. The time-track. A four-dimensional concept, having length, breadth, height and duration. Making up the time-track are the various "strips" of recorded data. Only a few of them are indicated.

We call this figure the "time-track." Imagine a man existing simultaneously in the time-space continuum which he has occupied or is occupying. The result would be a four-dimensional figure, having length, breadth, height and duration. It would begin at the point of union of sperm and ovum; it would terminate at present time. Looking backwards along its extent, we could see how this snake-like structure would loop back and forth between home and office, between home and school, between the crib and its mother's arms, and would finally disappear within the mother's body, fusing with her time-track.

If we were to cut a segment out of the time-track, at right angles to its long axis of duration, we could imagine that the figure would contain, among other things, perceptual registrations. Within the segment is a recording of vision, audition, taste, olfaction, vestibular function, touch-pressure, warmth, cold, cutaneous pain, muscle-tendon-joint sensibility, deep pain, deep pressure, organic sensation and visceral pain.* I suspect that to this list should be added the sense of bodily state—the sense of feeling happy or sad, well or ill, angry, fearful, etc.

These registered elements of sensation are associated by simultaneity or sequentiality of occurrence. For example, in this segment we might have the sight of a small, furry quadruped, the tactile sensation of warm fur, the pain of a scratch and the sounds "meow" and "kitty." During that segment of experience there is a complete equality of association: cat is meow is warm fur is pain is anger is fear. . . . This ability to perceive and record appears, I suspect, at a very early point on the time-track—possibly during the zygote stage, before nidation has occurred.

---

*This is the list of senses as given in Howell's *Textbook of Physiology*, W. B. Saunders Co., Philadelphia, 1947.

Note that these registrations of perceptual data are *not* meaningful; "meaning" results only after there have been repeated experiences with numerous associations. To a newborn baby light has no "meaning," except that it is associated with the fearsome experience of being forced out of a semi-parasitic intra-uterine existence into a strange new environment. Later light becomes associated with the time for activity and sounds, not-light with a period of quiet and sleep. Light reflecting from mother's face soon implies feeding—and so the process of associations and differentiations continues, becoming more meaningful with each new experience.

We assume that within each segment of the time-track there is a recording of all perceptive data of that instant; in addition, there is an analysis of the "meaning" of these data, arrived at by a comparison with previously-recorded data. Another probable recording is the action which was taken at that time. The segment containing the meow-kitty-scratch-pain recordings might also contain the action of pushing the cat away. The next time the stimuli fur-kitty-meow were presented there would be the information, "If you push fur-kitty-meow away, there will not be scratch-pain."

Consider again the diagram of the time-track, and observe that a person can manipulate the data recorded on his time-track in three different ways (Fig. 2). Incidentally, we consider these manipulations not as separate functions but as zones on a spectrum of function; the division is on the verbal, not the functional, level.

A person can *recall;* he can focus his awareness on each perceptic recording which was made at a specific segment in time, reviewing the integrated totality of *that* experience at *that* location on the time-track. Whether or not he can recall completely is a question which needs further study; for the purposes of continuing discussion let us assume that he can.

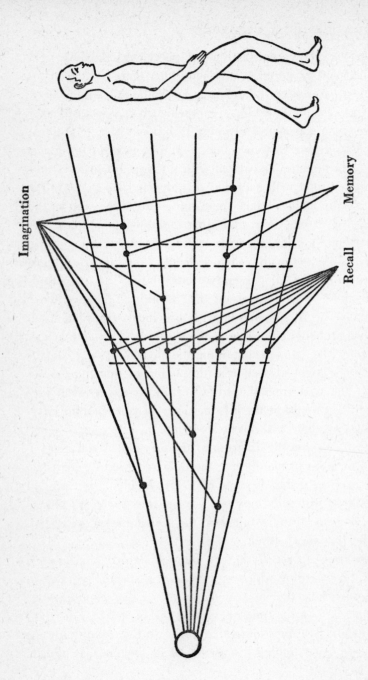

Fig. 2. Diagram illustrating the ways in which the data of time-track can be manipulated, i.e., selected and combined.

A person can *remember:* he can focus his awareness on the percept-recordings which are needed at the time he is remembering. For example, given the stimulus-question, "Did you graduate from high school?" the person takes the recollection of what he did, how he felt, what he saw, etc. on the day of his graduation, and from these he abstracts the single fact that he did graduate; he responds by saying, "Yes."

A person can *imagine:* he can take percept-recordings of one sense at one time on his time-track, combine it with another percept-recording from a different location and make a synthesis. For example, he can select the image of a girl with hair of unspecified color; he can select the color called "green" from his recollections of things green, and imagine a girl with green hair. By using "real" data from his experience, he can synthesize an "unreal" figment. What I call imagination, therefore, is "unreal" (i.e., has not occurred) in its synthetic totality; it is "real" insofar as the elements from which it is constructed have all been experienced at previous times.

There is a corollary function to imagination, one which uses the same synthesis-process, but for another purpose. We call it *prediction.* The function of prediction seems to be continuous and is not necessarily in the focus of awareness. It seems to be the necessary step which precedes action and is closely related to the phenomenon of choice.

Prediction seems to occur in this manner: a person becomes aware of stimuli in his environment and the stimulus pattern acts as a potential trigger for reaction. The experience is compared with similar experiences in the past, comparing the stimuli, the actions taken and the consequences. A series of predictions seems to be made, as if to say, "Past experience shows that I have had four similar experiences; I took a different course of action each time. With Action 1, I was hurt;

with Action 2, I was hurt; with Action 3, I had pleasure; with Action 4, I had neither pain nor pleasure. This time I shall choose to take Action 3."

It should be obvious that this function of comparison, evaluation and choice seldom reaches the level of awareness. The function seems to occur within a fraction of a second, too rapidly for "thinking" in the usual sense of the word. Moreover, a person can also make the choice of *not-action,* of negating a certain action without considering any alternative actions, as if to say, "I will not choose Actions 1, 2 or 4; instead I will do the opposite of Action 3."

It seems as if the ultimate prediction in each choice of action is "Death" or "Not-Death"—or, to express it another way, the possibility for continuing action or the impossibility for continuing action. In this sense of the word, "Death" (and we shall enclose the word in quotes to call your attention to the fact that it is being used in a specific sense) may include the loss of function of any part of the organism, as well as the cessation of function of the organism-as-a-whole. If a friend of mine dies or goes away, therefore, there has been "Death" for the part of my mind which deals with this friend; there is no possibility of future action with him.

The prediction of "Death" may be the last step in a long series of extrapolations. For example, a patient may react as if he predicts as follows: "If I have further therapy, I shall become friendly with the therapist; then I shall become dependent on him; then, if something should happen to him, I shall no longer be able to depend on him; then I might get sick and there will be no one to help me and I'll die. In order to prevent this, I must therefore discontinue therapy."

It has been noted that the more neurotic a patient is, the more extrapolations ending in "Death" he is apt to make. He might be able to be aware of several different choices, but if each of them implies ultimate "Death," he acts as if he is faced with an insoluble quandary. In other words, he fails to differentiate between a symbol for "Death" and death itself.

It has been observed that a characteristic emotional state obtains with different types of predictions. If a person predicts pleasure (in this sense, the possibility of continuing action), he acts in a manner which we call happy. If a person predicts "Death," he acts in a manner called sad. If he predicts conflict, he may become angry or fearful; anger seems to be elicited when there is a probability of emerging victorious from the conflict, fear when there is the probability of "Death" consequent to the conflict.

These are the emotional states which obtain in the interval between making the prediction and the actual occurrence of the predicted eventuality. There is another sort of emotional reaction which occurs when the prediction becomes an actuality: if the predicted consequence of a given stimulus-pattern was "Death" and the outcome was "Not-Death," a state of happiness seems to result; if the predicted outcome was "Not-Death" and "Death" occurred, sorrow seems to be the resultant emotion. Each of these emotions can be observed in a spectrum of intensity: sorrow seems to vary between disappointment and sobbing and weeping; happiness seems to vary between a state of well-being often imperceptible to the observer and, at the extreme, hearty laughter.

If this hypothesis is correct, then we can make certain inferences from the actions of the patient under observation. If a patient makes a remark, then smiles, we might deduce that he had predicted "Death" from making the remark; "Death" did not ensue, which meant that he could be happy. The nervous compulsive giggle which often characterizes certain neuroses and psychoses is, therefore, considered to be a manifestation of release from fear; from this, moreover, we can make inferences as to the situations which give rise to fear.

I should like to emphasize at this point that this hypothesis does not exclude other possible causes for laughter and happiness; this hypothesis is advanced as a possible explanation for *one* of the causes for laughter.

The spectrum of sorrow, extending from unobservable disappointment to overt weeping, is seen when a prediction of continuing action is demonstrated to be false. This is particularly noticeable in children, who tend to make more extreme reactions to stimuli than do the more repressed adults. A child asks for permission to perform an action—let us say, to stay up later than his customary bed-time. He seems to predict that he will be granted permission. When he is denied permission, thus making his prediction false, his response is often tearful sobbing.

In this hypothesis we follow the classification of the behaviorists, considering that there are four primary emotions: rage, fear, grief and love. Other so-called emotional states, such as excitement, shame, hate, annoyance, etc. are considered to be gradations of, or combinations of the primary emotions. We shall not consider the other so-called emotions, such as pleasure, joy, etc., because they do not seem to be aberrative. In other words, pleasure is not nearly so apt to change a person's behavior pattern as is fear or rage; in our therapeutic approach we find that if we can help the patient to understand his primary emotions, the emotion of pleasure takes care of itself.

For example, the state called excitement seems to occur when the person predicts danger of "Death" and relative safety from "Death" simultaneously. The excitement manifested by children in games in which they are scared is a case in point; the popularity of "horror movies," where people can observe frightening occurrences while still being aware of their own relative safety is another example of this.

The state of shame seems to result when a person does to someone else that which has been done painfully to him. We can cite as an example the man who was punished severely as a child; when he becomes a father he may punish his children, but the consequences of such an action would be a feeling of shame.

Hatred seems to be a state in which there is both rage and fear, and perhaps depends upon a pre-existing emotion of love. Hate is often engendered by a frequent restriction of activity and an inability to predict accurately. A good example of this is seen in the child whose parents frequently and without apparent reason restrict his choice of action; at the same time their decisions as to restriction or permission are so capricious and erratic as to be totally unpredictable to the child. He may be punished without warning, or he may be threatened *ad terrorem* without the predicted punishment ever being administered. In such a case the child usually develops toward his parents an attitude of fear, anger and suspicion which might be termed dislike, if not hate. The fact that he previously had learned to depend on his parents for love, attention and sustenance seems to make the negation stronger.

This hypothesis has been found to be useful in therapy because it gives us avenues of approach to behavior-patterns and emotional states which might otherwise be hidden. For example, the therapist might ask the patient, "Of what are you afraid?" and be unable to obtain information by such a direct approach. If he asks the patient to discuss excitement and exciting or exhilarating experiences, he soon obtains a good impression of what the patient's unrealized fears are and how they can be elicited.

A similar use can be made of the investigation of shame;

when the therapist finds what causes a shame-feeling to a patient, he gets a general idea of what was done to the patient. Again, this statement does not rule out the possibility that shame can be caused by other mechanisms.

To sum up, we find that prediction is a phenomenon which is an important one in the understanding of our patients and in leading our patients to a better understanding of themselves. Indeed, it is possible to define all neuroses and psychoses as states which result from making inaccurate predictions. The claustrophobe has a fear of enclosed spaces because he predicts that "Death" will occur if he enters or is forced to remain in such a restrictive environment. The manic is euphoric because he predicts that every eventuality will be good. The arthritic has stiffened joints because he predicts that it is dangerous to move unrestrainedly.

We must not forget, however, that predictions are only one link in the chain of activities. One must first have the experience which gives him the data on which he bases his predictions; in order to achieve therapy the patient should be able to examine his data, which are factual, and re-evaluate his predictions, which are fallacious. After this has been accomplished, the patient can then indulge in other courses of action than those which he had been rigidly following.

As a final word, it might also be pointed out that faith and belief are aspects of the phenomenon of prediction. We believe in those events which can be predicted with a high degree of accuracy and relative infallibility. We have faith in those people who give us information which is proved to be correct and who are predictable in their conduct.

The person who has "lost faith" or "can't believe" has therefore had two different types of experience with his predictions: at first he acquired sequences of data from which he learned to predict one course of events; later, he had another set of experiences which made his first predictions appear to be fallacious. The results which ensue seem to be either refusal to predict, which is a concomitant of apathy, or the constant prediction of danger—one aspect of chronic "free-floating" anxiety. The therapist can use this hypothesis in his search for traumatic experiences, remembering that he can look for the early experience which engendered one type of prediction and the later experience which negated it.

Idealization in general seems to be a type of prediction. The patient who is chronically disappointed because he fails to reach his highly idealized goals is acting as if he could not differentiate between a prediction and an actuality. This mechanism has been discussed in an illuminating manner by Johnson* as the idealization-frustration-despair syndrome.

We have found that patients can be helped superficially by making them more aware of their frequently fallacious predictions. Perhaps this is the essence of counseling—increasing awareness of prediction in order to be able to differentiate between a predicted reality and an actual reality.

The theory of prediction has been discussed at some length here because of its applicability to diagnosis rather than to therapy. It furnishes a viewpoint which might lead to better understanding of the reactions of our fellow men and is offered as a basis for further research. The discussion is, moreover, an exposition of work-in-progress, rather than an idea which has been completely worked out.

We have said that a person can manipulate the data of his time-track. This manipulation can—and does—also occur from without. Let us call the person the "I" and everything else the "not-I." There is a constant reaction between the "I" and the "not-I," each modifying the other. When the "not-I" delimits the "I's" choice of function, a learning process occurs

*Johnson, Wendell, *People in Quandaries*, Harper & Bros., New York, 1946.

which tends to channel the person's activities in future similar events. The learning process seems to be increasingly effectual with increasing pain and with decreasing ability to differentiate. When the person's ability to differentiate between the "I" and the "not-I" is at a minimum, as it seems to be during hypnosis and unconsciousness, his response-patterns are rigidly channeled.

It should be made clear that consciousness is *not,* as I see it, an either-or proposition. A more operational concept of consciousness is to say that it is like a spectrum, the quanta of which are differences perceived and acted upon. At the bottom end of the spectrum we would have no awareness of any difference whatsoever, a state usually called death; at the upper end we would have the state of complete awareness of every difference—and I suspect that we can only stipulate that state by means of extrapolation, that it is unattainable in actuality.

It follows, then, that when the organism is less-than-completely conscious, it is not differentiating completely; when it is not differentiating fully, it is less than completely conscious. In other words, any experience which restricts the ability of the organism to differentiate also produces a certain amount of unconsciousness.

Further, according to this concept we can say that unconsciousness occurs when the person is not permitted to differentiate. This happens, I feel, whenever a person is forced into an action not of his own choosing. The child who is told that he *must* go to bed responds by a decrease in his analytical differentiating abilities—during this state of attenuation of his analytical functions he is much more apt to act illogically and unreasonably, as most parents have observed.

It has been found that adhering to the concept of the mind as a spectrum of differentiation eliminates the concept of the reactive mind and the analytical mind. We have noticed that creating such an artificial dichotomy carries with it implicit value-judgments; the analytical mind becomes allied with the Powers of Good, while the reactive mind has been regarded as the dianetic concept of the Devil. It is possibly less confusing to speak of the reactive or analytical *zones*, with the understanding that there is no sharp line of demarcation between the two, and that they are merely labels for degrees of differentiation.

In therapy, it is our task to investigate those experiences in which there was decreased consciousness, decreased differentiation-ability. We assist the patient to survey a specific experience in the light of his total experience and to re-evaluate it. He becomes aware that "there was a time when I was constrained to do such-and-thus," and he learns to differentiate between that time and this, that person and this, those percepts and these. By so doing, he becomes able to choose among all possible actions; he no longer must have his choice limited to a single function.

An interesting and common failure of differentiation seems to be connected with the time-sense. Anthropologic studies have shown that humans have two different types of time sense, a lineal and a non-lineal. The lineal time-sense, characteristic of our society, relates time to exterior phenomena— the passage of day and night, the changing seasons, etc.—and identifies it with mechanisms such as the clock and the calendar. The non-lineal time sense, found in some primitive cultures, relates the passage of time to the individual's activities; the more activity which occurs, the more "time" which passes.*

*For a more complete discussion of this concept, the reader is referred to Lee, Dorothy, "Lineal and Nonlineal Codifications of Reality," *Psychosomatic Medicine*, 12; 89-97; March-April 1950.

The non-lineal time sense is seen among the Zuni Indians, whose language contains no past nor future tenses; they have a tense which expresses what actually occurred and another for what might have occurred or is occurring or will occur.

It is my impression that these two types of time-sense are both found in every human mind. The time-sense might be regarded as a spectrum, paralleling the spectrum of consciousness; when one is completely conscious, he has a lineal time-sense; when his degree of consciousness is attenuated, his time-sense becomes non-lineal.

The time-track, as graphically expressed, is an example of lineal time. Events are related to each other according to precedence and succession. During moments of pain and/or unconsciousness, however, the various percept-sensations are related only to those occurring within that segment of time, and the relationship thereby becomes less meaningful, tending toward identification, an exemplification of non-lineal time.

We could express graphically a fully-conscious, non-painful experience according to Fig. 3. We shall assume that a person has been presented with the stimulus-pattern of: "Would you like some ice-cream?" He compares the present stimulus with past experiences of ice-cream, predicts pleasure, and answers, "Yes, please."

Suppose now that our subject who is fond of ice-cream is subjected to a succession of experiences wherein he is kicked every time he eats ice-cream. After a while he will have established an association-pattern similar to the Pavlovian conditioned reflex, which might be expressed as in Fig. 3. His response to proffered ice cream would be a violent "No!", and if he was prevailed upon to eat some, he would be apt to notice a pain in the region which had been kicked.

In other words, it seems as if during a painful incident the progress of time has stopped; it is a moment of stasis, in

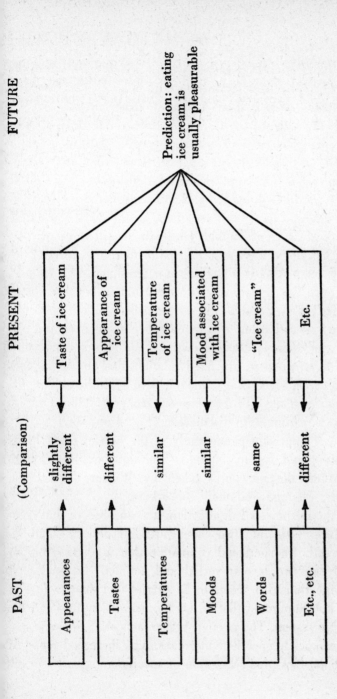

Fig. 3. Diagram illustrating a lineal time-sense.

which the relationships are only those which exist within the event. There are no relationships with other events; the painful moment acts as if it has a separate existence.

In therapy one of the things we endeavor to do is to take all the percept-sensations within a specific painful event or event of unconsciousness, separate them from each other, and establish a more appropriate relationship to other similar experiences. In so doing the patient learns that any given percept is likely to have been associated with pain at some time and with pleasure at another. He learns to differentiate: percept A has not always equalled pain, therefore reacting towards percept A as if it were pain is irrational.

Compare this hypothesis with the Hubbardian concept of "erasure." We see that a pain is diminished, not only by repetition to exhaustion but also by complete association and differentiation between the associations. We take a moment of stasis, in which there are fixed relationships among its constituent percept-recordings, make it fluid again by total re-experience—and the pain becomes a memory of Time Past instead of a restimulable discomfort. (Fig. 4 and 4a.)

Another approach to the study of the human mind in its functioning and dysfunctioning is from the viewpoint of communication—the viewpoint taken by Wiener, McCulloch, Shannon, Meduna and their co-workers.

For the purposes of description, we can observe that communication falls into two categories: interpersonal and intrapersonal. Interpersonal communication is carried on essentially on two levels: verbal and actional. Intrapersonal communication also seems to be carried out on two levels; neural and humoral—that is, via the nervous system and the endocrine system. The nervous system acts as if to carry specific messages to specific end-organs, e.g., increased tonus of specific muscles plus relaxation of specific antagonists in order to produce motion of an extremity. The endocrine system —and for this admirable concept I am indebted to Norbert Wiener—carries messages addressed "To Whom It May Concern." According to Cannon's theory, when a person is so stimulated that it appears necessary to run or fight, the adrenal medulla pours out epinephrine. This hormone circulating through the blood stream affects only certain potentially responsive functions.

It appears as if messages carried by hormones give rise to "emotions." A change in the blood level of circulating hormones alters the *milieu interne* of all body cells, and this in turn gives rise to the perception of a generalized bodily state labelled emotion. I suspect, though I know of no work to confirm it, that changes in blood hormone levels may produce changes in the permeability of some or all of the synaptic junctions between neurones.

At present our group is assuming that emotion is a means of potentiation of response: given a situation which requires a strong generalized response, the body can make this response more effectually when its functions are potentiated by hormonal changes. It also seems that an emotional state must be expressed in bodily action in order to restore the balance of functions; emotional states which are not expressed—or are repressed, if you prefer—are apt to lead to undesirable results.

Let me hasten to point out that I do not regard the foregoing categorization of communication as one of rigid accuracy. In intrapersonal communication there may be reactions which are purely neural or purely humoral; I suspect, however, that the majority of messages are carried by both systems. The main reason for setting up this dichotomy is for ease in speaking about it; I am aware of the neural elements in endocrine function and vice versa.

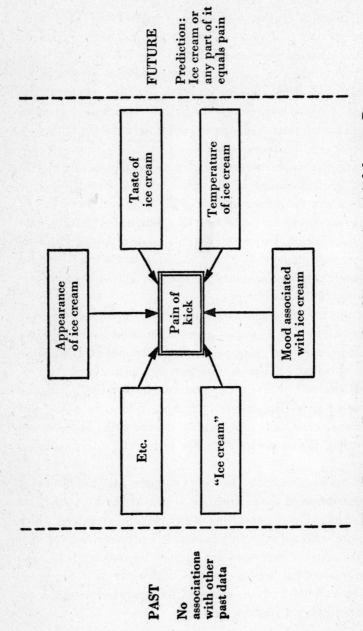

Fig. 4. Diagram illustrating non-lineal time sense in a painful event. Perceptions are related only to pain, which acts as a binding force.

**If a painful event
can be diagrammatically
expressed thus:**

**Then therapy process
results in this:**

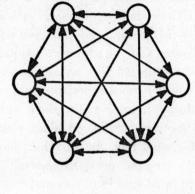

**plus association with other
similar perceptic data.
Note dispersal of pain.**

Fig. 4a

There is one important difference between neural and humoral messages—their communicability to other persons. I can tell you about my neural messages (i.e., how I think) with some degree of understandability, but it is well-nigh impossible for me to tell you about my humoral messages (i.e., how I feel). I can say that I see a red ball; you will look at the same object and agree that you also see a red ball. But if I say that I am angry, you do not feel my anger; you might infer that I am angry from previous experience with me in an angry mood, but you do not become angry along with me unless I give you some specific stimulus to elicit your own anger, which I, in turn, cannot feel. As Korzybski points out, emotions and feeling are on the unspeakable level.

This concept of inter- and intra-personal communication is brought out because of its therapeutic implications. As therapists, we are primarily concerned with disorders of intrapersonal communication; it is obvious that messages to the exterior world are only so good as the messages in the interior world of a person's own being. As an example of this you might consider the difficulties of patching up a quarrel between two people if one of them is acting in an almost psychotic manner.

It can be seen further that this viewpoint of communication might be used as a parallel classification of the psychoses and neuroses. The obsessive-compulsive person might be said to have a self-engendered message which says that he must perform a certain behavior pattern. The person with hypertension might have a message center which interprets every stimulus as one which should elicit the rage-response, plus the further injunction that this rage should be concealed as carefully as possible. The catatonic might interpret every outside stimulus as a command not to move—and so on.

In therapy, therefore, we must be careful to bring both of

these aspects of intrapersonal communication to the level of awareness. The patient should be assisted to consciousness of what he feels as well as what he thinks. He should be encouraged, during the therapy session, to express his feelings—not by verbalization but by *action*. If he feels so angry that he'd like to hit something, the suggestion is made that he pound on the couch. If he feels tearful, nothing is done to discourage his efforts to weep.

At the present time, it is one of my beliefs that therapeutic benefits are obtained when a person can choose what he will do. If he acts as if he *must* become angry whenever he is told to "go to hell," or if he *must* weep every time he feels rejected, there is compulsive behavior and a lack of free choice. In order for a person to be able to make a choice between two actions, he must be able to do either of the two alternatives. If he is going to choose whether to become fearful or not, he must be able to become fearful or not-fearful. He must know how to express himself either way. Further investigation might lead me to modify this belief, but until I have more data, I am assuming this as a postulate.

The inability to express appropriate emotional responses is notably common in our society. It is even more noticeable in the so-called "neurotic"; in the patient who is seclusive, inhibited and depressed, we can observe a marked inability to express emotion. An action-demanding stimulus can only change his degree of apathy. He cannot become angry; he cannot manifest joy; he does not weep—he is, in short, the Anglo-Saxon ideal of emotional atrophy.

One of our tasks as therapists, therefore, is to assist this type of individual to express his emotions in appropriate activity during the therapy session. Some techniques for accomplishing this task will be mentioned in the section under therapy.

It might be advisable at this time to point out that awareness of one's own emotional pattern frequently requires a meticulous evaluation of feelings. Emotions are seldom specific; they are more often confused and mutually inhibitory. For example, take the man who cries whenever he becomes angry and who becomes angry with himself when he cries. We might say that he has a confusion between anger and sorrow. Perhaps he has been taught in numerous fashions that it is shameful to cry, that men don't cry, that he is a sissy if he cries. He also equates anger with tears—he cannot, therefore, become angry because if he did so, he would cry and be ashamed.

We also observe profound differences between the way a person actually feels and the way he thinks he should feel. You can test this by having a patient repeat the words, "I am ashamed." He will usually report that he feels ashamed, and recalls various incidents in his life when he was ashamed. Then have him repeat, or say to him, "You ought to be ashamed." In many cases the response will change to one of anger. Since the extreme manifestation of shame is weeping, and the extreme manifestation of anger is aggressive action, we can see that there is a serious discrepancy between what he *does* feel and what he *should* (or he thinks he should) feel.

There is one more concept which should be defined and discussed—the concept of *reality*. In this hypothesis, reality has a rather specific meaning, and is defined as the totality of experiential data, with each datum being related to all others. Reality is not, according to this definition, a fixed state. Each new bit of experience, each new perception, is added to the store previously acquired, changing the pattern of the integrated totality. Reality is therefore a process, dynamic and ever-changing.

Reality is also a relative matter, varying with the number

of stimuli perceived. In any specific event there are numerous fluctuations in the environment which can be adequate stimuli for a bodily reaction. We might say that as the awareness of more and more stimuli increases, the reality of the situation increases.

It therefore follows that complete reality is a state rarely obtained. It is a human tendency to act as if unaware of parts of the perceptual field, or to make false-to-fact associations between various perceptions. The parent who becomes irritated at his children screaming happily during play is making a fallacious association between the screaming, which is factual, and his own pain, which may have been associated in the past with screaming.

However, there is a sort of reality in this association—an *internal* reality, the result of individual experience. At some time in this man's existence there *was* an association between pain and screaming; so this association of contemporaneous percepts was real at that time. There may also have been numerous other occasions when there was screaming and no pain, but this relationship is ignored, or abstracted, when he makes the response of irritation.

A person's internal reality, therefore, consists of a part of his total store of experiential data, with these being arranged in a particular, often static and fixed, pattern. Theoretically there should be a minimum of fixed patterns; each new experience as it is presented should alter pre-existent patterns, but such is seldom the case in the average "normal" human.

To give an example of this activity, let us take the child who learns about Santa Claus. He is given data about Santa Claus—a man with a white beard, who wears a red suit, and who brings toys to good little boys and girls at Christmas time. The child has "proof" of the existence of this figure: his parents told him there was a Santa Claus, he has seen pictures of Santa Claus, and there were the results of Santa's activities, the toys under the tree. Some of the data is a little doubtful, of course: if his only means of entrance to a home is via the fireplace chimney, how does he get into an apartment? But the "proof" cited before suffices—Santa Claus is a part of the child's internal reality.

Then new data is acquired; one of the child's more cynical playmates informs him that "there ain't no Santa Claus." He cites other "proof," and data previously overlooked is now considered. After a period of confusion the child alters his internal reality to the concept that Santa Claus is another one of those inaccurate stories his parents tell him. As he matures, more data is acquired and integrated until he gradually has the usual adult concept of an anthropomorphic symbol of the spirit of Christmas, of good cheer and, in our society, of commercialism.

There is another facet of reality in this process of acquiring intellectual maturity—the concept of *external* reality, which is defined as the total store of experiential data of the group in which a person lives, with the data arranged in a particular pattern, as before. Internal reality is individual and experiential; external reality is general and consensual. And in our society, a most important criterion for sanity is the conformity between an individual's internal reality and the external reality of society.

I have found this viewpoint of reality a helpful one, productive of constructive thinking. It clears up the impasse of the patient who does not "face reality" by delineating the reality which he is incapable of "facing." It seems to me that a psychotic looks upon external reality, finds it threatening, and turns his psychic eye on the only reality left to him—a portion of his past experience wherein he was relatively safe.

As a sidelight to this, I can report that several catatonic patients have informed me that they haven't been born yet.

This concept also throws a light on the problem of the therapist; it is his task to assist his patient to re-examine his past experiential data for any fallacious associations. The data is factual and not aberrating *per se;* the associations formed by simultaneous or sequential occurrence, wherein coitus is equated with "I'm dead" or a headache with "it's a fine boy" or the ringing of a bell with food, need re-evaluation in the light of total experience.

─────── IV ───────

IN CONDUCTING a session of dianetic therapy, the patient's comfort is given first consideration. As in classical psychoanalytic technique, the patient is asked to lie down in a quiet, darkened room. All influences which can keep him in too great a state of awareness of his present-time surroundings are held to a minimum. He should be asked to loosen any constricting garments, and should be advised that a full stomach or a full bladder may be a distraction. Occasionally it is advisable to suggest to your female patients that they wear "slacks"; the necessity of re-adjusting skirts to prevent any immodest exposure may act as a deterrent to getting into an event or to acting out some emotional pattern.

The therapist should also try to prevent any possibility of distractions; if there is a telephone in the room, the bell should be silenced or muffled. It should be understood that outsiders will not be permitted to disturb the session for any but emergency reasons. If there are any observers, they should be warned to be silent.

It should be pointed out that there is no danger in not following these suggestions, but experience has shown that greater therapeutic benefits can be obtained by so doing. In the therapy session the patient is asked, in a sense, to ignore his present environment and to concentrate on a previous experience. Any factors which make or keep him aware of present time seem to prevent him from re-experiencing the sensation of a past event. The patient is nonetheless aware of present time, aware that he is recalling an event from his store of past experiences. One of the reasons for therapeutic benefit is, I feel, the comparison between the past and the present, and the re-evaluation of past fixed responses in the light of present total knowledge. We therefore try to assist the patient to a state where he is *equally* aware of the present and the past, with neither being ubiquitous.

Once the patient has taken his position on the couch, he is asked to close his eyes; it appears that opening of the eyes tends to make him overly-aware of present time, so for that reason sessions are conducted with the patient's eyes closed throughout. He is told that the only requirement is a free expression of his thoughts and feelings, that he should give the first answer which occurs to him when a question is asked, without making any attempt to censor the response or evaluate it for good sense.

In his book, Hubbard placed stress on getting the patient into the hypnoidal state which he calls "reverie." It has since been found that the majority of people go into this state automatically during their efforts to recall. Rather than discuss reverie *per se*, I shall give those methods which are used for starting a session; it will be observed that the signs of the hypnoidal state (fluttering eyelids, deepened respirations, relaxation) become manifest spontaneously.

The method of counting, as mentioned in the book *Dianetics,* has been abandoned.

Another method, contributed by a student of Yoga, is as follows: ask the patient to imagine that all his thoughts, all his being, are concentrated at a point an inch back of the center of his forehead. Allow him a few seconds to direct his attention to this point, then suggest that he imagine himself falling backwards and downwards until he reaches the earliest moment of discomfort which is now available to him. Give him a few more seconds to experience this, then ask, "What is the first phrase which occurs to you?" With this phrase the session is begun.

Perhaps the most frequently used method is that of asking the patient to recall some recent event when he enjoyed himself. It is better to choose some situation in which there is activity, such as swimming, dancing, or eating a good meal, rather than a sedentary pleasure such as reading. The patient is asked to recount all his perceptions which occur within a short and specific span of time. It is required that the patient use the present tense in speaking of these events; experience has shown that by so doing one recovers more of the perceptic content. The therapist likewise uses the present tense in his questions. (See Appendix for questions to ask to assist recall.) This pleasure-moment is recounted a half-dozen times or until the patient has apparently recovered all the content of the event. He should be encouraged to *re-experience* rather than merely to verbalize the sensations. If the pleasure-moment includes swimming in cold water, the patient should be asked to try to feel the cold again. If some person with whom he is swimming has made a remark, the patient is asked to try to recall the exact intonations of the speaker's voice. If the patient was swimming, he should be asked to feel the movements in his arms and legs.

This method is a good one to use when introducing the technique for the first time. When the patient learns that he can, to some extent, feel again what he once felt and hear again what he once heard, the therapist points out to him that that is what is meant by "returning." He then requests the patient to return to the earliest available moment of discomfort, and the session goes on.

Once the patient has been acquainted with the process of "returning," a session can be started in a less formal manner. One way is to ask the patient what he is thinking about. Suppose the patient says, "Sleep." The therapist asks him to discuss sleep, to tell about its good and its bad aspects. Ultimately the patient will make a remark that demonstrates a relationship between sleep and pain or painful emotion; the therapist then directs him to return to the event wherein pain and sleep occurred simultaneously. After exhausting the pain of this event he is asked to return to an earlier event, and so on until the end of the session or until the patient seems unable to recover any earlier events.

Still another way of starting a session is to inquire if the patient has any discomfort. If so, he is asked to recall previous times when he had similar discomfort. The therapist will notice that a patient will have a certain pain in response to certain characteristic stimulus-patterns, and he will endeavor to have the patient become aware that he is and has been following a rigid stimulus-response pattern. Every effort is made to help the patient to arrive at this awareness himself; if the therapist explains it to him, there seems to be less therapeutic benefit obtained.

Or the therapist may note that the patient frequently or invariably assumes a certain position on the couch; he will then ask the patient to go to a time when he lay in that position or when he saw someone else lying in that position.

This gambit is used most often when the patient takes a position similar to that of a corpse as it is laid out in a coffin. Making the patient aware that he is re-dramatizing a death will often enable him to return to that death and release its emotional content.

Still another method is to observe the characteristic verbal expressions which a patient uses, either spontaneously or in answer to certain types of question. These phrases may be used as entering points for therapy. The therapist asks the patient to repeat one of these phrases and to give the associations with the phrase. Before many repetitions the patient usually makes some sort of association, such as a past experience in which this phrase was important; he may also develop a mood or a sense of discomfort and the situation can be developed from there.

The responses of various patients to the opening of a session fall into rather well-defined categories. A patient may lie inertly on the couch, avowing that he feels nothing, hears nothing and goes no place. Or he may make the same avowals, but may also appear tense and rigid, or he may grimace or squint, or he may move his feet in an agitated manner. The third type of patient will report rather promptly that a sense of discomfort, either localized or generalized, has developed.

We make the following interpretations of these types of conduct. The inert patient is, we believe, prevented from returning because of an atrophy of the recall-process. In other words, his response-pattern is one of "remembering," wherein an abstraction is made of each event; the aspects of the event which have an indifferent survival value are ignored, left outside the zone of focal awareness. The aspects of the event which have an extreme survival value are likewise overlooked; it is as if becoming aware of these would be dangerous or painful or both. For this type of patient we concentrate on pleasure-moments for at least the first half-hour, until he can realize that it is possible to re-experience an event of the past with impunity.

The agitated patient who denies that he is returning has, we believe, approached an area of disturbance, but is unable to recall the contents of the event because *he may not*. It seems as if all of us do as we do because we must, and that we deny ourselves abilities because we are commanded to do so. It is as if there are commands laid down in the reactive, sub-analytical portion of the mind which say, "Don't remember anything or you'll die." With this grim alternative as part of his internal reality, the patient will find it difficult to recover any recollections whatsoever.

For this type, besides using pleasure-moments as a form of reassurance, we also try to have him recognize the essential silliness of such a belief. It *is* a belief, incidentally; if a person acts as if it were dangerous or even fatal to return to an event, he must believe it, even if he stoutly denies that he has any such belief. We may ask him for a flash answer (i.e., for the first answer which occurs to him, no matter how he evaluates the correctness of the answer) and inquire, "What would happen to you if you felt something?" If he says, "Die," the therapist asks, "Do you believe, logically and analytically, that you would die if you felt something?" He does not, of course; such a belief is not logical or analytical, and he will usually smile at the nonsensicality of it. The therapist may also ask, "Would you have any objection to feeling something?" to which the patient usually replies, "No." In most cases the patient shortly thereafter reports some sort of discomfort.

With the third type of patient, the one who feels discomfort and who recalls what occurred, we have less difficulty. Our minor aim in therapy, in fact, is to get the first two types of patient to the point where they can react as does the third type. Note, if you please, that I said *can* react—not will react. We shall frequently see patients who have the idea that it would please the therapist if they manifested a certain pattern of conduct. In their efforts to be cooperative and to do what the therapist obviously thinks is best, they will describe recollections which seem suspiciously lacking in authenticity. These patients do not do this with malice aforethought; it seems instead to be a manifestation of obedience to some such command as "Do what the doctor tells you and you'll get better." We also see a similar response in patients who have been trained in a less specific manner to be compliant to the wishes of established authority.

Experience has taught us that as a patient becomes less aberrated, less compulsive and less sorrowful, his abilities to recall also improve. Instead of vaguely remembering that someone said something that he didn't like, he will recall almost verbatim what a certain person said on a specific occasion and that the remarks were inappropriate or inaccurate, in his opinion. The ability to recall in this manner, as if re-hearing the person's words, is referred to as "sonic recall" in Hubbard's book; it is supposed to be one of the results of successful therapy. I do not believe that it should be considered as a *goal* of therapy, however, nor should it be stressed enough so that the patient gets a feeling of being unfortunate because of the absence of this method of recall. Remember that some people act as if they *must* be unfortunate, and that it might be dangerous for them to be able to hear with their mind's ears, or to see with their mind's eyes.

Let us suppose that we have the patient lying on the couch with his eyes closed; he has been asked to return to a moment of discomfort and he reports that he is aware of an uncomfortable sensation, either localized or generalized. What do we do then?

By questioning we try to assist the patient to a complete awareness of the moment in time during which he had the discomfort. He reaches the awareness by describing and re-experiencing, so far as he can. If there was a pain in his right wrist, he is asked to feel the pain again. If at the same time the wind was blowing and mussing his hair, we ask him to feel the sensation of his hair being mussed. By inquiry and request he is assisted to recall everything which he perceived during the period of time when he had the pain in his wrist.

But the perceptions of the event are not sufficient; he must also be assisted to recall his reaction to the event. We ask, "How do you feel? What are you doing? What would you like to do? What mood goes along with this experience? Are there any other moods besides this one?"

Finally we inquire as to the meaning of the event. We treat the verbal content of the event as if the statements made had to be obeyed. The patient may have obeyed them or not— but we ask him how the statements could be obeyed. For example, someone might have said, "I feel bad." We ask the patient, "What does that mean? What does it mean to feel? What is bad?"

We encounter some highly interesting ideas when the patient is permitted to analyze the literal meanings of words and phrases in this fashion. The responses elicited often startle the therapist with their highly personalized nature. The literal interpretations of the phrase, "I feel bad," can be discovered to include "I feel wicked," "I am evil," "I have a dysfunction of sensation," "I am emotionally repressed," etc. Furthermore, patients are frequently observed to behave, either verbally or actionally, as if they were obeying all of these meanings of the command.

The session is terminated at a point where the patient is comfortable. If the therapist is working on an appointment basis, he should be careful not to introduce his patient into any new situation near the end of the session, as it is highly uncomfortable for the patient to be sent out of the office with a painful incident in full restimulation. I suspect that it might be definitely dangerous in some cases.

The Hubbardian method of terminating a session is to ask the patient to take a deep breath and "come up to present time." The question, "How old are you?" is thrown at the patient; if he gives a number less than his actual age, he is asked for his actual age and told again to breathe deeply and come up to present time.

My preference is for the method of making the patient aware of himself in his present surroundings: "Now, notice how you feel—the position in which you're lying—notice the position of your hands—notice how your limbs feel—notice the sounds in the room—my voice—become aware of where you are—what day it is—open your eyes."

In order to illustrate a method of handling a painful event in therapy, let us consider the case of a woman whose chief complaints include backache, disinterest in coitus, and an inability to "get started." She presents a picture of lack of initiative, passivity and propitiation—verbally anxious to please but with actions tending to resist change. There is a lack of emotional expressivity, an apathy which sometimes borders on melancholia.

She lies down on the couch with a sigh, and says, "I don't know what's the matter with me today. I just had to force myself to keep this appointment. I didn't want to come at all."

THERAPIST: How do you feel?

PATIENT: Oh, all right, I guess. (Shifts position of hips on couch.)

(T.) How does your back feel?

(P.) It's been aching a lot lately. It feels just like I've been beaten.

(T.) Answer the next question with a name, please—the first name that occurs to you. Who beat you?

(P.) (No answer for about 5 seconds.) I don't remember any beatings.

(T.) What was the first name you thought of?

(P.) Mother—but I can't remember that she ever *beat* me.

(T.) Did your mother ever punish you?

(P.) I suppose so. (Mirthless giggle.)

(T.) Let's see if you can recall a time when your mother punished you. What do you suppose that she might have punished you for?

(P.) I haven't the least idea.

(T.) Supposing that you were a mother and had a little girl who did something to deserve a punishment. What would the little girl have done?

(P.) Maybe spilled some ink on the carpet.

(T.) Where did your mother used to take you to punish you?

(P.) In the bathroom.

(T.) See if you can recall what the bathroom looks like. Can you see it?

(P.) Yes, vaguely.

(T.) What does she hit you with?

(P.)   A hair-brush.

(T.)   What do you suppose it sounds like to be hit with a hair-brush—like this? (T. slaps his leg to imitate the sounds of a spanking.)

(P.)   (Becomes generally tense, shifts position of hips on couch.) That's it.

(T.)   Let's go to the time your mother is spanking you. Listen to the sound. Where is she hitting you?

(P.)   On my bottom. (Nervous giggle.)

(T.)   Can you feel it?

(P.)   No.

(T.)   What does your mother say?

(P.)   I don't know.

(T.)   Repeat that phrase, please.

(P.)   (Repeats.) I don't know . . . I don't know . . . I don't know. . . .

(T.)   Let's imagine that a little girl is getting a spanking because she spilled ink on the carpet. What do you suppose the mother would say while she was spanking her. Some sentence with "I don't know" in it?

(P.)   She might say, "'I don't know what's the matter with you lately."

(T.)   See if you can remember how it feels to be spanked. Repeat the words, "I don't know what's the matter with you."

(P.)   (Repeats; makes rotary motions with feet.)

(T.)   Can you feel the spanking?

(P.)   No.

(T.)   What would happen to you if you could feel it?

(P.)   That would be a sign I was getting better.

(T.)   What would happen if you got better?

(P.)   Oh, that would be heavenly.

(T.)   How does a person get to go to heaven?

(P.)   If he's real good.

(T.)   What does he have to do first?

(P.)   He has to die.

(T.)   Notice, please, what you just said. You said that it would be "heavenly" if you could recall the pain of a spanking; then you said that you'd have to die in order to go to heaven. Does that mean if you felt the pain of this spanking that you'd die?

(P.)   Of course not.

(T.)   All right, you can feel it. Notice what position you're in.

(P.)   Mother is sitting down on the edge of the bathtub and is holding me across her lap. I can see it.

(T.)   Are you looking at yourself or are you inside yourself?

(P.)   I can see myself.

(T.)   Try to get inside yourself and feel the discomfort of the spanking. Notice how it sounds. (Slaps leg again to imitate sound.) Can you feel it?

(P.)   It hurts! (Voice tone suggests resentment.)

(T.)   What does she say?

(P.)   "I don't know what's the matter with you lately."

(T.)   Anything else?

(P.)   I don't know—I'm stopped.

(T.)   Repeat the word "stop."

(P.)   (Repeats.)

(T.)   Put it in a sentence.

(P.)   Stop your crying.

(T.)   Does your mother say, "Stop your crying in 1951"?

(P.)   Of course not.

(T.)   Does she say, "Stop repeating the words in this incident"?

(P.)   Why, no.

(T.)   You can continue. Go over those words again, please.

(P.)   "I don't know what's the matter with you lately. Stop your crying."

(About 10 repetitions.)

(T.)   How does your bottom feel?

(P.)   Sort of a burning sensation—it's getting stronger.

(T.)   What else does she say?

(P.)   I don't know.

(T.)   Who says, "I don't know"?

(P.)   My mother.

(T.)   Are you your mother?

(P.)   I guess I am, sometimes.

(T.)   Where is your mother today?

(P.)   Why, she's dead—I told you that.

(T.)   Are you dead?

(P.)   No.

(T.)   Are you your mother—logically and analytically?

(P.)   (Laughs.) Of course I'm not.

(T.)   You can see the difference between yourself and your mother. Now, what does she say?

(P.)   (Appears to hesitate.)

(T.)   What's the matter?

(P.)   I just don't seem to be able to say it again. Isn't that silly?

(T.) Do you suppose she might have said, "Don't do that again"?

(P.) That's it! "Don't ever do it again." (Repeats this phrase a half-dozen times.)

(T.) Let's go back to the beginning of this scene. Feel your mother holding you. Notice what you're looking at.

(P.) I can see her blue dress.

(T.) Feel her hitting you. Notice the sound. What is she saying?

(P.) I don't know what's the matter with you lately. Don't ever do it again. Now, stop your crying." (Repeated in a flat tone of voice.)

(T.) Is that the way she says it? "Stop your crying"? (Therapist uses an exaggeratedly flat voice-tone, a parody of the patient's.)

(P.) No. (Laughs.)

(T.) Try to imitate her voice tones. Repeat it again, please, and feel her hitting you.

(P.) (Repeats about 10 times.)

(T.) How does your bottom feel?

(P.) Much better.

(T.) How is the backache?

(P.) That's gone, too. Do you suppose that there could be any connection between this spanking and my backache?

(T.) What do you think?

(P.) There might be, at that.

(T.) Let's consider what your mother says: "I don't know what's the matter with you lately." Suppose that you had to obey that statement as if it were a command: what would you do?

(P.)   Well, I wouldn't know what was the matter with me—or with you, either, I guess.

(T.)   What do you say when somebody asks you to do something?

(P.)   (Sighs.) I usually say "yes."

(T.)   You don't "no"?

(P.)   That's right—I don't.

(T.)   Do you have to not know—either K-N-O-W or N-O just because your mother doesn't know?

(P.)   No—I can make up my own mind.

(T.)   How about that phrase, "Don't ever do it again"? What does that remind you of? Are there any things that you don't like to do more than once?

(P.)   Oh, lots of things—I didn't want my second child very badly.

(T.)   You can see how this phrase might apply to you. Do you have to obey this command?

(P.)   No.

(T.)   You can "do it again" or not, as you wish. Let's go through this again, and tell me if anything else occurs to you.

(P.)   (Repeats.)

(T.)   How do you suppose that you sound when she spanks you?

(P.)   I suppose I cry.

(T.)   Try to imitate the sound of your crying.

(P.)   Waaa . . . waaa . . . waaa . . . (Laughs heartily.) That sounds so silly.

(T.)   Make that crying sound again, please.

(P.)   Waaa . . . waaa . . . (Yawns and stretches.)

(T.)   What does your mother say?

(P.)   "Stop that crying."

(T.)   You can cry if you want to, can't you?

(P.)   Sure. (Yawns again.)

(T.)   Let's go through this again.

(P.)   (Repeats 4 or 5 times.)

(T.)   How do you feel now? Any discomfort?

(P.)   No, I feel good. (Yawns and stretches again.)

It should be pointed out that this is not a verbatim report of an actual session; it is, rather, a condensation of several sessions with a typical patient. This patient had been in therapy for some weeks and was conversant with the idea of giving uncensored and unevaluated associations.

Notice the use of simple, vernacular language and the stressing of simple, apparently obvious differences. There is a definite reason for such simplicity. The human mind may be regarded as a spectrum of functions, the increments being the number of differences of which the person is aware. In every event there is an infinite number of differences which can be recognized (i.e., perceived and reacted upon); the more differences recognized, the more "conscious" the person is, and the more intelligent he is. On a low level where only a few differences are recognized, a person behaves as if he were a vegetable; on a slightly higher level, like an animal; on a still higher level, like a moron; on an even higher level, he would behave like an intelligent human. We notice also that this concept refers to *total* behavior, where differences are recognized *actionally* as well as verbally; a person may speak intelligently yet act idiotically.

In dealing with aberrated conduct we are dealing with a moronic level of consciousness and differentiation-ability; the therapist therefore speaks as if to a moron.

It has been observed that patients in therapy do not regard these differentiations as obvious nor act as if they realized them. The recognition of a ludicrously obvious difference (e.g., I am not my mother) often is an important therapeutic achievement.

The questions which the therapist asks, while they appear superficially to be simple, are not; they are purposeful, and the purpose is to elicit responses. It is assumed that everything a patient says and does during a session is related in some way to the event which he is trying to recall. A question is asked and an answer is elicited; the answer may be verbal or it may be actional, and the therapist regards the answer as pertinent. Moreover, the suggestions and requests which the therapist makes are assumed to be effectual—if not immediately, then ultimately.

Let us go over this session in greater detail, point out the assumed significance of the patient's responses and how they were utilized by the therapist.

(P.) *Lies down, sighs and says, "I don't know what's the matter with me today. I just had to force myself to keep this appointment. I didn't want to come at all."*

It has been observed that deep breathing and sighing seem to accompany the effort of re-directing one's attention from the past to the present—a concomitant of "coming up to present time," in dianetic terminology. From the patient's remarks, the therapist infers that the patient is in a reaction pattern acquired in the past, and that this pattern is presumably one in which she was forced to do something.

(T.) *How do you feel?*
(P.) *Oh, all right, I guess.* (*Shifts position of hips on couch.*)

Note the conventional verbal response to the question; the action, on the other hand, is a more revealing response which suggests discomfort of some sort. Occasionally we see a shifting of the hips as an action-token of coitus; with the next question the therapist tries to find out if there could be another association.

(T.) *How does your back feel?*
(P.) *It's been aching a lot lately. It feels just like I've been beaten.*

Knowing the history of backache, the therapist asks this question. The answer, which might be considered as hyperbole in ordinary conversation, is considered to be a literal comparison—a memory, rather than a simile.

(T.) *Answer the next question with the first name which occurs to you. Who beat you?*
(P.) (*Delayed answer.*) *I don't remember.*

By asking for a "flash" answer, the therapist seeks information from the reactive, rather than the analytic, level of mind function. It is a similar process to that utilized in word-association tests. The delayed answer is thought to indicate the presence of associated pain and/or emotion. This sort of question is asked rapidly, as if trying to surprise the answer out of the patient. An answer which is delayed is deemed to be analytical, therefore relatively valueless to therapy.

The therapist takes for granted that there is an incident of this nature. To one who has not had experience with this type of therapy, this may seem like suggestion. However, the initiate soon discovers from the patient's behavior whether he has located an area of disturbance; if the therapist has guessed wrongly, the patient will soon demonstrate it by disinterest.

(T.) *What was the first name you thought of?*
(P.) *Mother—but she never* beat *me.*
(T.) *Did your mother ever punish you?*
(P.) *I suppose so.* (*Giggle.*)

The therapist suspects that the patient has censored her response, that there was a "first answer," but that she evaluated it as unreasonable in her current estimation of reality. The mirthless giggle, which is recognizable if not describable, is believed to be an indication of fear; it seems as if fear is sometimes released in laughter. The therapist concludes that there is fear of punishment (a more acceptable word than "beating") of such a degree that even talking about it produces a fear reaction.

(T.) *Let's see if you can recall a time when your mother punished you. What do you suppose she might have punished you for?*

(P.) *I haven't the least idea.*

(T.) *Supposing that you were a mother and had a little girl who did something to deserve punishment — what would the little girl have done?*

(P.) *Maybe spilled some ink on the carpet.*

The therapist, having identified the incident which is presenting itself, is now trying to get the patient into the recollection of the event. Knowing there is fear connected with it, he makes a circuitous approach: i.e., uses "suppose" and "might," words which allow the patient to feel that this could be "imaginary" rather than real. The patient shies away even from this gentle approach, so the therapist shifts her to a safer, more successful viewpoint—that of the mother. The reason for the punishment is of minor importance; the patient's ability to stipulate a reason indicates that she is approaching the incident.

(T.) *Where did your mother used to take you to punish you?*

(P.) *In the bathroom.*

(T.) *See if you can recall what the bathroom looks like. Can you see it?*

(P.) *Yes, vaguely.*

(T.) *What does she hit you with?*

(P.) *A hair-brush.*

(T.) *What do you suppose it sounds like to be hit with a hair-brush — like this?* (*Slaps leg.*)

(P.) (*Becomes tense, shifts position.*) *That's it.*

(T.) *Let's go to the time your mother is spanking you. Listen to the sound. Where is she hitting you?*

(P.) *On my bottom.* (*Giggle.*)

(T.) *Can you feel it?*

(P.) *No.*

The therapist continues trying to help the patient to bring up all the background details of the scene. It seems advisable to have the patient oriented in space-time; the reality is thereby increased. The actual means of punishment is important only insofar as it is another detail in the picture which the patient is building up.

The therapist imitates the sound of a spanking in order to make the total picture of punishment more clear. Judging from the increased tension and agitation, it is an effectual means of re-stimulating the event of punishment.

The therapist calls the patient's attention again to the idea that she is supposed to be experiencing a specific event; he also continues trying to develop the complete perceptic content of the incident, especially the pain and sorrow. The report that the patient cannot feel the discomfort is interpreted as indicating that she is still somewhat removed from the incident.

(T.) *What does your mother say?*

(P.) *I don't know.*

(T.) *Repeat that phrase, please.*

Here is an attempt to find out whether there is something in the verbal content which increases the threat to survival or which acts to deny knowledge of the content of the scene. Notice that the patient's answer is taken literally: the therapist does *not* infer that the patient doesn't know— he assumes that she is answering his question directly. By having her repeat the phrase, fatiguing what might be called the "I-don't-knowness" of it, she is helped to a closer contact.

(P.) *(Repeats.)*

(T.) *Let's imagine that a little girl is getting a spanking because she spilled ink on the carpet. What do you suppose the mother would say while spanking her? Some sentence with "I don't know" in it?*

(P.) *She might say, "I don't know what's the matter with you lately."*

Again, with the device of "let's imagine" and the positing of a hypothetical little girl instead of the patient, the patient is enabled to add to the content of recollection from a vantage point of comparative safety from pain. Note that the patient brings up a sentence very similar to the one she first used at the beginning of the session. It can usually be predicted that this will occur.

(P.) *(Repeats; makes rotary motions with feet.)*

This is interpreted as confirmatory evidence of pain associated with the event. The patient is not feeling (is not "aware" of) the pain, but the presence of pain in the incident under review necessitates some sort of action to diffuse it or express it. The wriggling of the feet is characteristic of a pain present in the field, but outside of the focus, of awareness.

(T.) *Can you feel the spanking?*
(P.) *No.*
(T.) *What would happen to you if you could feel it?*
(P.) *That would be a sign I was getting better.*
(T.) *What would happen if you got better?*
(P.) *That would be heavenly.*

The therapist now tries to get at the cause of the lack of pain-recall. A frequent reason for this is the verbal threat of death, either explicit or implicit. It is noteworthy that patients seem to shy away from verbal threats more than they do from the actual pain connected with the incident; in other words, the fear of a death-threat is greater than a fear of pain.

(T.) *How does a person get to go to heaven?*

Recognizing the death-threat implicit in "heavenly,"

(P.)   *If he's real good.*

(T.)   *What does he have to do first?*

(P.)   *He has to die.*

(T.)   *Notice what you just said. You said it would be "heavenly" if you could recall the pain of a spanking; then you said you'd have to die in order to go to heaven. Does that mean if you felt the pain of this spanking that you'd die?*

(P.)   *Of course not.*

the therapist endeavors to bring it to the patient's attention. This is a typical example of the identification process which characterizes the reactive level of mental function. In bringing this false-to-fact equivalence to the level of the differentiating function of the mind, the threat evaporates. Notice also that the patient has a confusion between being "real good" and death. This should be noted for exploration at a later session, as should also the incident or incidents containing the death threat and the circumstances under which the patient learned about Heaven.

(T.)   *All right, you can feel it. Notice what position you're in.*

(P.)   *Mother is sitting down on the edge of the bath-tub and is holding me across her lap. I can see it.*

(T.)   *Are you looking at yourself or are you inside yourself?*

(P.)   *I can see myself.*

A permissive positive suggestion, intended to counteract the effect of phrases which restrict knowing, feeling, etc. The report of seeing herself indicates that there is still a threat in this incident; it is as if the patient was trying to avoid the threat by being exteriorized and out of contact with the danger. This phenomenon is manifested very frequently in the schizoid type of personality, where there is poor contact with reality, but is often found elsewhere.

(T.) *Try to get inside yourself and feel the discomfort of the spanking. Notice how it sounds. (Slaps leg.) Can you feel it?*
(P.) *It hurts! (Tone of resentment.)*

The patient is encouraged to feel the discomfort while she is pushed further into the scene by an imitation of one of the sounds associated with spanking. The pain is recalled, and the scene is now complete in its important elements.

(T.) *What does she say?*
(P.) *"I don't know what's the matter with you lately."*
(T.) *Anything else?*
(P.) *I don't know — I'm stopped.*
(T.) *Repeat the word "stop."*
(P.) *(Repeats.)*

This illustrates the literal obedience to a command uttered in a painful incident. It is as if the patient, when she encounters a restrictive suggestion, must obey it in whatever action-modality she is using; she is recalling, the command says "stop," so she stops recalling. The patient usually manifests the presence of a command first by obeying it; when asked why, she will then put the command-word into an appropriate context as she does here. If she does not give a clue to the command-word, it can usually be obtained by having her repeat the preceding phrase; then asking for "what's next?"

(T.) *Put it in a sentence.*

(P.) *"Stop your crying."*

(T.) *Does your mother say, "Stop your crying in 1951"?*

(P.) *Of course not.*

(T.) *Does she say, "Stop repeating the words in this incident"?*

(P.) *Why, no.*

(T.) *You can continue. Go over those words again, please.*

(P.) *(Repeats.)*

The therapist is testing for the completeness of the phrase. After one has used this technique for a while, he develops a sense of appropriate dialogue, and whenever the words which the patient brings up do not seem complete, he looks for additional phrases. Experience shows that if there are no additional phrases, the patient will insist vehemently that there are none. One should be circumspect in using this device, however, as it might be placing undue influence on the type of patient who is anxious to please the therapist. Once the sentence has been obtained, the therapist assists the patient to differentiate—in this case, to differentiate between "then" and "now" and between "stopping" and "stopping crying." It is my practice to establish differentiation and realization of such emotion-restrictive commands whenever I encounter them. In this patient, who was notably lacking in emotional expressivity, it was especially advisable.

(T.) *How does your bottom feel?*
(P.) *Sort of a burning sensation—it's getting stronger.*

Notice that the therapist keeps feeding the patient's own terminology back to her —he uses the word "bottom" rather than another synonym for the gluteal region. The report that the discomfort is increasing is interpreted as a closer contact with the incident and as an indication of the validity (in the therapeutic sense) of her recollections. This does not mean that the therapist believes that the incident is actual and real; he assumes, however, that this is a statement of the patient's internal reality at this time in the therapy process. This spanking scene might be an abstraction of numerous similar scenes, and perhaps the patient must review a prototype scene before she can distinguish among the various incidents.

(T.) *What else does she say?*

(P.) *I don't know.*

(T.) *Who says, "I don't know"?*

(P.) *My mother.*

(T.) *Are you your mother?*

(P.) *I guess I am, sometimes.*

(T.) *Where is your mother today?*

(P.) *Why, she's dead—I told you that.*

(T.) *Are you dead?*

(P.) *No.*

(T.) *Are you your mother, logically and analytically?*

(P.) *(Laughs.) Of course I'm not.*

(T.) *You can see the difference between yourself and your mother.*

This is a technique which has been found to be useful in handling the well-known phenomenon of identification. It seems to give the patient the opportunity to use his analytical powers and to differentiate between a reality and a false identification. If the patient's mother says, "I don't know," and the patient also does not know, it implies that she has identified herself with her mother. Not only has she failed to differentiate between herself and someone else, but she has also failed to differentiate between her mother's verbal report and her own actions—in this case, the action of knowing. The therapist is demonstrating to the patient that here is a statement to which the patient is responding as if it were a factual command which had to be obeyed, and that such a response and such an evaluation and such obedience are not necessarily the only ways in which she can react. The patient is shown that *she has a choice of actions* and that she doesn't have to be in the state of "I don't know" unless she so chooses. This, of course, is not the only event in which the patient identifies herself with her mother —but by reducing the pain connected with the identification, we insure that there is one less event of confusion. The therapist ends this exercise in differentiation with another permissive positive suggestion, an assurance that the patient *can* differentiate.

Here is another example of obeying a command, with the patient unaware that she is telling the therapist the content of the command. Patients will frequently comment that they don't see how the therapist can figure these things out, when actually the patient is reporting, literally and unequivo-

(T.) *Now, what does she say?*
(P.) *I just don't seem to be able to say it again. Isn't that silly?*
(T.) *Do you suppose that she might have said, "Don't do that again"?*
(P.) *That's it! "Don't ever do it again." (Repeats.)*

cally, the mechanisms which are deterring her. Notice also that the patient does not take the exact words which were offered to her, but modifies them slightly to suit herself.

(T.) *Let's go back to the beginning of this scene. Feel your mother holding you. Notice what you're looking at.*
(P.) *I can see her blue dress.*
(T.) *Feel her hitting you. Notice the sound. What is she saying?*

The process of adding to the perceptic content of the scene continues. The therapist is trying to tie up an established datum—the feeling of being held—with new visual data. He directs her attention again to previously established data.

(P.) (*Repeats words in a flat tone of voice.*)
(T.) *Is that the way she says it?* (*Parodies the patient's voice-tones.*)
(P.) *No.* (*Laughs.*)
(T.) *Try to imitate her voice-tones. Repeat it and feel her hitting you.*
(P.) (*Repeats.*)

Inasmuch as the voice-tones are a part of the meaning of a statement, it is advisable to have the patient become aware of the probable emotional overtones in her mother's voice during this scene. The device of exaggeration to the point of humor is used here: by getting the patient to laugh, it is as if she is released from some of the terror associated with the words and their intonations.

(T.) *How does your bottom feel?*

(P.) *Much better.*

(T.) *How is the backache?*

(P.) *That's gone, too. Do you suppose that there could be any connection between this spanking and my backache?*

(T.) *What do you think?*

(P.) *There might be, at that.*

The decrease in the pain suggests that most of the content of this scene has been recovered. The patient is trying to make an association between an injury of the past and a chronically-present pain; further, she asks for confirmation of her interpretation. The therapist evades this; it is my belief that the patient's own intepretation has much more therapeutic value than the therapist's—it is derived from her experience, not his. The patient has already been influenced by a painful and restrictive experience to make a non-valid association; if she wishes to re-evaluate the associations among her data, she should be permitted to do so without the external influence of the therapist's approbation.

(T.) *Let's consider what your mother says: "I don't know what's the matter with you lately." Suppose that you had to obey that statement as if it were a com-*

Here is a continuation of the process of interpretation; notice that the therapist *does not* interpret for the patient, but that he leads her to make her own inter-

mand: what would you do?
(P.) *Well, I wouldn't know what was the matter with me—or with you, either, I guess.*
(T.) *What do you say when somebody asks you to do something?*
(P.) *I usually say, "yes."*
(T.) *You don't "no"?*
(P.) *That's right—I don't.*
(T.) *Do you have to not know—either K-N-O-W or N-O—just because your mother doesn't know?*
(P.) *No—I can make up my own mind.*

pretations. Incidentally, it is seldom that a patient can realize that he has been acting as if he has been obeying engram-commands until it is called to his attention. It is this failure of realization, I believe, which indicates the aberrative qualities and effects of such literal obedience. I feel that this realization should be developed until the patient seems to be thoroughly aware of the false reality which has been created for him by force of circumstances. If it requires more time than is indicated in this report, I believe that the therapist should spend as much time in this process of guided interpretation as he thinks necessary. It will be observed that as therapy progresses the patient can analyze and interpret with increasing ease and understanding.

Notice also that the therapist considers the *sound* of "know" or "no," rather than the different *meanings* of these homonyms. Apparently a patient can and will obey the sound of a command, rather than its meaning; it is a literal, rather than a meaningful, reaction. Clinical observation has shown that "I don't know" is frequently found in the overly compliant and suggestible person, and it has been found to be especially prominent in cases of promiscuity.

(T.) *How about that phrase, "Don't ever do it again"? What does that remind you of? Are there any things that you don't like to do more than once?*

(P.) *Oh, lots of things—I didn't want my second child very badly.*

(T.) *You can see how this phrase might apply to you. Do you have to obey this command?*

(P.) *No.*

(T.) *You can do it again or not, as you wish.*

More interpretation, with the patient seemingly realizing that this phrase is applicable to her sexual-procreative activities. The therapist continues to use permissive suggestions and to point out that the patient has more than one alternative from which to choose. Learning to disobey a command is, I believe, the first step in becoming freed from restricted conduct; the next step is the awareness of other alternatives of reaction not concerned with the command.

(T.) *How do you suppose that you sound when she spanks you?*

(P.) *I suppose I cry.*

(T.) *Try to imitate the sound of your crying.*

(P.) *Waaa . . . waaa . . . (Laughs heartily.) That sounds so silly.*

The therapist is trying to get all the content of this event, including the patient's own audible response. It seems as if most persons equate the sound of their crying with the presence of pain; they hesitate to cry because it might be painful. It is, I feel, therapeutically necessary for a patient to be able to cry, for reasons which will be discussed later. By demonstrating, even on this superficial level, that it is possible to cry without having pain the degree of emotional inexpressivity is lessened. The response, "That sounds silly," is interpreted as a realization that crying is not necessarily painful.

It is also a moot point as to whether or not there was any unexpressed sorrow in this event. It has been my experience that rage is more apt to be the emotional residuum which should be released. To me it seems that the crying in this scene is a concomitant of actional impotency, rather than the grief resultant from deprivation.

(T.) *Again, please.*

(P.) *Waaa. (Yawns and stretches.)*

This illustrates what is, to me, one of the most interesting phenomena of dianetics —the yawning and stretching which occurs when a painful incident has been reviewed and the pain disappears. Yawning is interpreted as a sign that the "unconsciousness" which has been associated with the incident has been dissipated, while the stretching seems to indicate relaxation of the muscles which had been tensed as part of the attitude of fear which accompanies painful experiences. It has been observed that the patient who does not yawn does not obtain as much relief from the session as does the patient who yawns copiously. It has also been observed that, when a person in everyday life has some trivial discomfort such as a headache, the pain will be noticeably ameliorated following yawning. The physiology of the yawning process deserves thorough investigation.

(T.) *What does your mother say?*
(P.) *"Stop that crying."*
(T.) *You can cry if you want to, can't you?*
(P.) *Sure. (Yawns.)*
(T.) *Let's go through this again.*
(P.) *(Repeats.)*
(T.) *How do you feel now? Any discomfort?*
(P.) *No, I feel good. (Yawns and stretches again.)*

The therapist is making a final check-up of the effectiveness of the patient's review of this incident. The discomfort has disappeared, the yawning and stretching have been manifested: the incident is deemed to have been reduced. From here the therapist can go to an earlier situation—an earlier punishment or an earlier occurrence of one of the phrases, sounds or discomforts of this incident. For example, he might ask the patient to go to the first time she cried, which would probably be found at birth. If she was sent to the first occurrence of the slapping sound, she might go to the moment of birth where the obstetrician is slapping her in order to initiate breathing. Or the slapping sound might remind her of a similar sound during coitus.

If, on the other hand, the pain had not disappeared,

the therapist might have investigated other data observed during the recounting. For instance, at one point the patient said, "It hurts!" in a voice-tone suggesting resentment. The therapist might have called the attention of the patient to this feeling and led her to realize at whom the anger was aimed. It might even be necessary to have her express her anger in action, according to the method described in the chapter on emotion. It might also be necessary to look for unexpressed grief.

The therapist, in taking a patient through a session such as this, finds that he is constantly evaluating for himself the patient's responses and that he must be on the alert for simple, innocent-appearing phrases which might be associated with the patient's behavior-pattern. He does this by assuming that everything the patient says or does has a survival value to him. The therapist recognizes that there may be other reasons for the patient's behaving as she does, but he considers that all behavior offered during a therapy session is engramic (i.e., learned via a painful experience) until proved otherwise. It is only in this manner that the full possibilities of this hypothesis and therapeutic method can be realized.

I find that the problem of "resistance" becomes clearer and easier to deal with when one assumes that a patient behaves as he does because he must obey a specific command. With this postulate we have a more definite target at which to aim, and it has been my experience that the problem of resistance is relatively minor with this form of therapy.

Assuming that the patient is manifesting literal obedience is a time-saver in another way: there is less time spent in rationalizing of behavior. Contrast this method of dealing with the patient who "doesn't know" with the method of explaining such ignorance on the basis of an Oedipal reaction; it is my opinion that dianetics offers a more operational and effectual methodology.

It should also be pointed out that a simple situation such as this, containing only three sentences, gives the therapist numerous opportunities for further investigation of the patient's personality pattern. He can assist the patient to a further understanding of the concept of Heaven, of the necessity for crying or not crying, of the value-judgment implicit in the word "good." He can help the patient to a recognition of her mother as a person, instead of an idealization, confused and irrational, of a mother as a doting parent at one moment and a stern executioner at another. The material which can be obtained by dianetic methods is so profuse that the problem is not what to investigate but what not to investigate.

THE DIFFICULT CASE

———————— V ————————

Not all patients will give the same sort of response as that described in the previous chapter. Some, when asked to return to some incident of their past, can give only an abstraction of what happened; they can remember only the focal-area of the scene, and can recall nothing of the background. If asked to return to a dinner-party, for example, a "difficult" patient might remember that he did go to a dinner-party some time or other, but he can't remember when it was or what he ate when he got there. He might remember that he had a good dinner, but he cannot visualize the appearance of his plate or re-experience the taste of his food or recall any of the conversation.

We say that such a person has an occlusion of his recall-abilities, and part of the therapy process is the dissolution of this blockage. We feel, as a result of clinical experience, that the better a person's recall-abilities are, the less apt he is to be neurotic or to have any of the so-called psychosomatic illnesses. We also observe that as an illness (either of function or of structure) improves, the ability to recall and re-experience improves *pari passu*.

Occlusion of recall is a recognizable entity; there is also a state of pseudo-occlusion, and the two states should be differentiated.

It is advisable for the therapist to give the patient some idea of how he should react in therapy. The patient should be informed that he is expected to give the first answer that occurs to him to any question which he is asked. We are looking for the reactions of the reactive level of the mind, which seems to respond much more rapidly than the analytic portion. The patient should be asked not to evaluate the response nor to censor it in any way; if he feels like saying, "Go to hell," he should say it without restraint. He should also report sensations of discomfort, even if they are vague and almost imperceptible. He should become aware of his feelings, and tell the therapist of any changes in mood or affect.

The manner in which the patient is asked to conduct himself in therapy is, in short, the exact antithesis of the training-pattern which the general semanticists hold up as the ideal. The disciples of Korzybski, when asked a question, are supposed to pause in order to obtain sufficient time for thalamico-cortical integration. We encourage our patients to respond as rapidly as possible in order to tap the region of the mind wherein the emergency, non-analytic functions seem to lie, for it is within this region that we find the failures of differentiation and the roots of aberrated behavior.

At the same time, one should be careful not to permit the patient to give only what he thinks the therapist wants. The psychoanalysts are very familiar with the patient who free-associates beautifully, yet obtains a minimum of therapeutic

benefit from his analysis. We see a similar situation in dianetics, where the patient brings up "engrams" with the greatest
of ease, yet manifests no beneficial change in his reaction-
pattern.

One way in which we can get a clue as to whether the
patient is obtaining benefit from therapy or is merely trying
to please his therapist is to inquire about the reality of the
material which he brings up. Does this seem real? Do you
think that this actually happened? Do you feel that this is
definitely not imaginary? If he gives negative responses, it
is probably better to consider only those events which happened since the age of three, when memory (as opposed to
recall) seems to put in its appearance. This area should be
worked until the patient has an unequivocal feeling of the
reality of his memories; after this we might try to reach
occluded areas or go earlier.

The area of dubious reality in dianetics is, of course, the
prenatal. Some patients seem to recall events occurring in
an environment which strongly suggests the intra-uterine
state: they report that their surroundings seem to be dark,
warm and moist; they feel crowded and unable to move
freely; they feel discomfort over their entire bodies. When
such is the report, it is my practice to refer to such an environment as "prenatal," and to tell the patient that he may
consider this as "prenatal" if he so desires. I should like,
however, to see some definitive and unequivocal evidence of
the existence of prenatal recollections before I regard this
concept as anything more than a postulate on which to base
a therapeutic approach.

One of the factors which prevents me from accepting the
concept of "prenatal" recollections whole-heartedly is that
a number of patients act as if they regarded the prenatal
area as a sanctuary of escape from the rigors of postnatal

reality. These patients cannot recall the details of an event which occurred a half-hour before the session; when asked to return to some painful event which occurred within a few months of present time, they writhe on the couch and manifest some sort of emotional disturbance, such as a tremulous voice or generalized bodily tension. On the other hand, when asked to return to a "prenatal" event, they relax happily and bring up reams of "recollections" of what happened two hours after conception.

There are, admittedly, several explanations for this sort of reaction. It might be that the prenatal portion of a person's life appears to be happy and safe as compared with more recent periods of suffering. It might also be that the "prenatal area" acts as a screen upon which the patient can project an imaginative explanation for his present disturbances.

Still another reason—and I believe that it is especially important in our society—is that the prenatal portion of a person's life is the one area wherein he has no responsibility for his actions. Everything which occurs is done *to* him, not *by* him, and any feelings of guilt are thereby obviated. Some of the undeniable therapeutic benefits which have been obtained from considering a "prenatal engram" might well have resulted from the patient's construction of a guilt-free explanation for his behavior. I feel, however, that the therapy process should not stop at this point; self-absolution from guilt still implies that a feeling of guilt exists. It is better if the patient can be assisted to the point where he regards his past experiences as factual, without carrying an emotional burden into his present-time existence.

Perhaps I should make it clear that I am hesitant in accepting the validity of *early* "prenatal" recollections only. The immediately pre-birth and birth portions of a person's time-track seem to be easily accessible, easily recallable, and the recollections seem at the present time to have a high degree of authenticity.

Let me put it this way: I do not believe that the value of dianetics rests solely on the concept of recollection of prenatal percept-recordings. It is an intriguing hypothesis and, if true, offers an explanation for phenomena otherwise inexplicable. It is my practice to use the concept as one basis for therapy, but to reserve judgment of its objective reality.

I tend to suspect "prenatal" recollections of having less-than-maximum validity especially when the patient has visualizations of the extra-uterine environment; other suspicious signs to me are the failure of the patient to yawn and stretch and the tendency to feel the discomfort which is suggested by the verbal content of the event, rather than the sort of discomfort which is structurally possible for the individual to sense at that stipulated time.

To give an example: the therapist might ask for an "age-flash" by saying, "Answer this next question with a number, the first which occurs to you. How many days past conception is this?" The patient answers, "Five." The therapist asks, "What do you feel?" to which the patient replies, "I have a headache."

The study of embryology teaches us that the zygote, on the fifth day post-conception, is still in the morula stage, and the neural cleft has not yet appeared; there is no such structure as a head which could ache. Moreover, on further examination of this incident, the patient will ultimately report that his mother says, "I have a headache."

If, on the other hand, the patient reports a feeling of generalized discomfort and pressure, and is aware of a floating sensation, he is reporting sensations which are structurally possible (if not probable) at this stage of development; we accept this report as at least suggestive of "prenatal" recall as defined.

(Classical dianetics labels these two types of response as "command somatics" and "actual somatics," respectively; a command somatic is one of the criteria of being in the "valence" of the person who verbalizes the discomfort.)

It might be pertinent at this time to discuss a tentative explanation of this sort of manifestation. It is my impression that in the course of his lifetime, a person has perceived sensations and has recorded memories of total darkness, a generalized feeling of moisture on the skin, generalized pressure, a floating sensation, headache, etc. He has also heard the words, "I have a headache," and has probably said them himself. With these bits of data he can construct, using the function called imagination, a scene in which all these elements seem to appear simultaneously, even though the various sensations were not originally perceived in a single specific segment of time. In this scene the concomitant discomfort can be reduced or eliminated by recounting and repetition to exhaustion. The "validity" of this is in the response—the elimination of discomfort—and the objective reality of the "recollections" can await further testing.

Judging from the responses of patients when reviewing painful scenes in youth or adulthood, the more complete and accurate the recollections are, the more therapeutic benefit will be obtained from the review. If a patient reviews his father's funeral and recalls how his father looked in the casket, he will, after continued recounting, be freed from a sense of sorrow and loss. If, on the other hand, he returns to the time when he looks at his father in the casket and seems to see him as he looked five years previously, the degree of relief from sorrow seems less. Nevertheless, *some* relief—or therapeutic benefit—is obtained. In other words, an imaginary or asynchronic scene can be reviewed with profit; reviewing a real or synchronic scene seems to produce greater benefits.

Here let me interject an idea of the functions of memory, recall and imagination, as we define them. In recall, one re-experiences every perception which occurred at the time of the event; to express it another way, recall is total memory of a specific segment of time. Memory is the recall of only part of one's perceptual experiences in a less specific segment of time. Imagination is a synthesis of real bits of data from various segments of time into a construct which could possibly exist. Imagination deals with the Might-Have-Been, not the Was. When the imaginative process is directed towards the future, it becomes prediction; directed towards the past, it becomes a substitute for memory or recall. Imagining during sleep is called dreaming.

Many forms of psychotherapy deal with imagination, in the sense of the word used here. Jung, in particular, dealt with concept-structures which were not synchronic in reality —i.e., imaginary. His work has demonstrated that a patient can be benefited to some degree by exercise of the function of imagination, although it appears that the means is too frequently substituted for the end.

In my observation of patients, I find that imagination is a method of living and a means of escape from reality, as well as a necessary function for prediction and constructive creation. Some patients—and they are usually labelled as "difficult"—seem to have lost their abilities to recall and even find it difficult to remember. With this type of patient we must endeavor to help him to recover his sense of reality about past experience by leading him over the route of Imagination.

To give an example of this let us take a typical remote-from-reality patient and show how he can be encouraged to imagine. Let us assume that this man acts as if discouraged about a lack of therapeutic gains, and as if angry at his inabilities to recall and remember incidents of past experience.

PATIENT: I just can't seem to get into anything.

THERAPIST: Let's consider the idea of "getting in"—what conditions or acts could be described by those words?

(P.) Oh, lots of things.

(T.) Let's name a few—circumstances where not getting in might be unpleasant.

(P.) Maybe not getting into a fraternity at college.

(T.) Anything else?

(P.) Maybe "not getting in" during coitus.

(T.) Who do you suppose would complain more about this failure to get in—the man or the woman?

(P.) I don't know—either one, I guess.

(T.) Who do you think would be more apt to complain?

(P.) The man, I suppose.

(T.) All right, let's imagine a scene where a man and a woman are having intercourse and the man is complaining about not getting in. Can you see it?

(P.) (Chuckles.) Yes, he's disgusted.

(T.) What do you suppose he might be saying?

(P.) I can't imagine.

(T.) Let's try to write a little scene—like a "soap opera." We want to make this good and dramatic. Here we have a scene where a man and a woman are trying to have coitus, and the man can't get in. What do you suppose that the woman might say?

(P.) "That's good enough for you—I didn't want to anyhow."

(T.) And then what might happen?

(P.) Then the man would say, "Go to hell," and he'd roll over and go to sleep.

(T.) Let's go over this script again—who would be the first one to speak?

(P.) I don't know.

(T.) It would have to be either the man or the woman, wouldn't it? Who do you suppose it would be?

(P.) All right, let's make it the man.

(T.) And what would he say?

(P.) "Damn it, I can't get in."

(T.) Continue, please.

(P.) Then she'd say, "That's good enough for you—I don't feel like it anyhow." Then he says, "Go to hell!"

(T.) Repeat those words, please—"I don't feel like it."

(P.) (Repeats.)

(T.) Who says those words?

(P.) The woman.

(T.) Are you a man or a woman?

(P.) A man, of course.

(T.) Then anything this woman said wouldn't have to apply to you, would it?

(P.) I guess not.

(T.) Repeat the words again, please.

(P.) (Repeats.) I don't feel like it.

(T.) If these words hurt you, where would they hurt?

(P.) I don't have any idea.

(T.) Suppose these words were said by your mother

and father before you were born—how do you suppose
that you'd feel about them?

(P.) I suppose I'd get angry.

(T.) How do you feel when you're angry?

(P.) I just tighten up all over.

(T.) Try to imagine that all-over tight feeling and repeat those words.

(P.) (Repeats.)

(T.) Can you get that tight feeling?

(P.) Yes.

The therapist can now proceed to develop this incident as
described in the previous chapter. He has some verbal content
to work with and the patient has reported a sense of discomfort. The patient is asked to continue to repeat, adding any
other phrases which occur to him, directing his attention to all
sensations and emotions which occur to him, until the discomfort is diminished or eliminated.

I do not claim that this "event" ever occurred as "recalled" by the patient. He may be reviewing a prototype of
several scenes, or he may be projecting his own feeling of
anger and discouragement, creating a plausible fictional explanation for his inadequacy. Nor would I deny that the
therapist in this scene might be accused of asking leading
questions which might encourage fictionalization and fantasy.
That is the purpose.

This seems to go along with the concept expressed on p.
79—if a person is to be able to choose between two alternatives, he must be able to perform both of them. In other
words, in order to differentiate between "imagination" and
"reality," a person must be able to imagine and be aware
that he is imagining; he must also be able to recall what is

real and be aware that it really happened. The technique as described seems to help accomplish this differentiation; by voluntarily imagining he learns to recognize imaginary events. This is of value because the patient who has been punished as a child for failure to differentiate between "imagination" and "the truth" acts as if he is afraid to imagine. A rediscovery of his ability to imagine without being punished for this mental activity helps further to reduce internal tensions.

Finally—and I feel that this is highly important—when we utilize this technique, the patient reports that he feels better, and observations confirm it.

Let us analyze, as we did in the previous chapter, the significance of the patient's remarks and the purpose of the therapist's suggestions.

(P.) *I just can't seem to get into anything.*
(T.) *Let's consider the idea of "getting in"—what conditions or acts could be described by those words?*
(P.) *Oh, lots of things.*

The therapist regards this phrase not so much as a statement of present difficulties but more as a token-phrase labelling an entire behavior-pattern. He therefore asks for similar "I can't get in" situations so that the patient may become aware that he is following a rigid pattern.

(T.) *Let's name a few—circumstances where not getting in might be unpleasant.*
(P.) *Maybe not getting into a fraternity at college.*
(T.) *Anything else?*

The patient names first a situation which is possibly real; the therapist chooses to disregard this because he feels that the patient needs to develop his abilities to im-

(P.) *Maybe not getting in during coitus.*

(T.) *Who do you suppose would complain more about this failure to get in—the man or the woman?*
(P.) *I don't know—either one, I guess.*
(T.) *Who do you think would be more apt to complain?*
(P.) *The man, I suppose.*

(T.) *All right, let's imagine a scene where a man and a woman are having intercourse and the man is complaining about not getting in. Can you see it?*
(P.) *(Chuckles.) Yes, he's disgusted.*
(T.) *What do you suppose he might be saying?*
(P.) *I can't imagine.*

(T.) *Let's try to write a little scene—like a "soap*

agine. If the imaginary scene could not be developed, the therapist would return to the real one.

The therapist is testing for the degree of remoteness from an actual situation: the patient cannot "suppose what would" happen, but he can "think what would be more apt" to happen. It can be seen that the second statement is further removed from actuality than is the first.

The therapist moves the patient to an even more remote viewpoint by asking him to "imagine a scene." By stipulating that the scene is imaginary, implying unreality in the usual sense of the word, the patient acts as if he feels safer—if it's imaginary, he feels as if he won't be hurt. We infer, as before, that the chuckle indicates the association of fear with the concept of not getting in, as well as evidence of what the patient thinks is humorous.

Again the therapist leads the patient away from actual

opera." *We want to make this good and dramatic. Here we have a scene where a man and a woman are trying to have coitus and the man can't get in. What do you suppose the woman might say?*

(P.) *"That's good enough for you—I didn't want to anyhow."*

(T.) *And then what might happen?*

(P.) *Then the man would say, "Go to hell," and he'd roll over and go to sleep.*

(T.) *Let's go over this script again—who would be the first one to speak?*

(P.) *I don't know.*

(T.) *It would have to be either the man or the woman, wouldn't it? Who do you suppose it would be?*

(P.) *All right, let's make it the man.*

(T.) *And what would he say?*

(P.) *"Damn it, I can't get in."*

(P.) *Then she'd say, "That's good enough for you —I don't feel like it any-*

reality. By putting the imaginary scene into the framework of a radio "soap opera," which typifies the unreal and the "corny" in our society, the patient can imagine freely without fear of a real pain— as if it really didn't happen. The effectiveness of the dramatic approach has been well demonstrated by Moreno in his psychodrama.

The patient continues to shy away from anything resembling actuality; we infer that his inability to state who speaks first indicates this. The therapist gives him a simple choice, and the patient assigns the first speech to the man. If he had said the woman was the first speaker, the scene would be developed in a similar fashion, although the content would undoubtedly be different.

Here we observe an opportunity for transition between stipulated unreality and *how." Then he says, "Go to hell."*

(T.)   *Repeat, "I don't feel like it."*

(P.)   *(Repeats.)*

(T.)   *Who says those words?*

(P.)   *The woman.*

(T.)   *Are you a man or a woman?*

(P.)   *A man, of course.*

(T.)   *Then anything this woman said wouldn't have to apply to you, would it?*

(P.)   *I guess not.*

(T.)   *If these words hurt you, where would they hurt?*

(P.)   *I don't have any idea.*

(T.)   *Suppose these words were said by your mother and father before you were born —how do you suppose you'd feel about them?*

(P.)   *I suppose I'd get angry.*

(T.)   *How do you feel when you're angry?*

(P.)   *I just tighten up all over.*

possible reality. The words "I don't feel" can act as a restrictive command; being uttered by a woman there is a greater possibility for differentiation, inasmuch as the patient is a man. Practice in differentiation is carried out on the simple level discussed previously. Notice also that the patient has changed the words from "I didn't want to" to "I don't feel like it"; this is a common occurrence and is interpreted as a search for more accurate recollections.

The therapist asks a question in a form which has proved useful, although it was ineffectual in this case.

The therapist now leaves the stipulated imaginary event and tries to develop a situation complete with feeling of discomfort. There is still the possibility that the scene which the patient will bring up may be partially imaginary—but he has been able to approach a real area of disturbance more closely by this circuitous route.

With the developing of a feeling of discomfort after an approach through imagination, we feel that the patient is well on his way to complete recollection of a specific experience. Once the patient feels the discomfort—*his own discomfort*— he seems to be reassured, as if to say, "Well, this isn't so bad; guess I can stand this pain long enough to find out what else is going on." It is only when there is some specific threat of death, either explicit or implicit, that a patient seems averse to recalling an incident; pain, even though severe when first experienced, does not seem to be as great a deterrent to recollection.

One further point should be made: this sort of patient seems to be dissociated from reality. He acts as if his own internal reality, the recordings of his past experiences, were so horrifying that he would be injured even if he remembered it. The act of imagination, on the other hand, is relatively safe; it is an assumption of our society that that which is imaginary is not real. We have noted before, however, that one can imagine only with the data he has experienced and recorded, and therefore any "imaginary" scene contains enough elements of reality to give the therapist a starting point from which to develop memory and recollection.

We note also that it appears to be relatively safer to imagine a traumatic event happening to someone else than it is to imagine oneself undergoing pain. The therapist in using the "radio script" technique helps the patient to construct a simulacrum; the patient can realize his fears by projecting them on his imaginary (yet partially real) scapegoat.

Another type of case which requires the utmost in therapeutic acumen and ingenuity is that of the patient whose emotional expression has been thwarted. Before we discuss the methods of dealing with this problem, a discussion of the basic concept of emotion as it is used in this book is necessary.

My understanding of emotion is that it is a state of the entire body; it is not localized nor identified with any specific region. As a concomitant of emotion, there is probably a marked change in the blood level of one or more hormones. In their extreme states, we can distinguish four emotions, which can be tabulated as follows:

Emotion	Hormone associated with the state	Active manifestation of the extreme state
Rage	Epinephrine	Fighting; aggressive action
Fear	Epinephrine?	Flight; possibly passivity, such as is seen in fear paralysis
Grief	Unknown	Crying; sobbing; lachrymation; tension of trapezius muscles; feeling of having a "lump in the throat," manifested by increased and/or difficult swallowing.
Love	Sex hormones?	Coitus

It is admitted that the assigning of specific hormones to specific emotional states is probably inaccurate; I do so only because I know of no other way in which a generalized bodily state can be obtained. It could possibly be that an emotional state would cause over-production of a histamine-like substance, which would in turn cause a generalized alteration of bodily state—but this too would be a hormone-like effect.

It has also been observed that the release from an emotional state may have a characteristic manifestation. Fear seems to be released in laughter—especially laughter from the vantage-point of safety; the dramatists have known of this mechanism, utilizing it in "comic relief." Grief, when released by crying, seems to leave one with a sort of philosophic acceptance of one's loss. I am not yet prepared to discuss the release of rage-tension or love-(sex-)tension. I have often noticed, however, that a patient who reviews several sexual incidents during the course of a session will urinate copiously at the end of the session. Could there be a correlation between this observation and the effect which sex-hormones have on water retention?

There are numerous other bodily states, often called emotions, which can be assigned to one of the four emotional states which I stipulate. For example, annoyance seems to be part of the spectrum of rage. Shame seems to be part of the spectrum of grief. Anxiety seems to be associated with fear. Hate might possibly be a mixture of love, rage and fear. It is difficult to deal with these finer nuances of feeling in our present methods of therapy; in fact, by helping the patient to a better understanding of the extreme emotional states, the less extreme states seem to take care of themselves.

In the therapy of those conditions which are characterized by emotional dysfunction I utilize a concept which I have mentioned before: in order to choose between following a specific behavior-pattern and not following that pattern, one must be able to follow it and not follow it. For example, to be able to choose between walking and not walking, a person must be able to walk; if he cannot walk because he has been deprived of his legs, he has no choice in the matter.

In the area of emotions, a person should, I feel, be able to choose between expressing anger and not expressing anger, between weeping and not weeping. But in order to do so he must be able to become angry and to express it, and he must be able to weep unrestrainedly. It appears as if it is more difficult to express anger than it is to become angry, more difficult to weep than it is to feel tearful.

In our society with its Anglo-Saxon set of value-judgments, the expression of emotional states is rather frowned upon. The strong, silent, poker-faced man is the ideal, rather than the emotionally labile, emotionally expressive type seen among Mediterranean peoples. In our society, however, this "ideal" state is achieved by *repression* of emotions, rather than by choosing not to express emotions. There is a subtle, yet important, difference between these two activities. If one represses emotions, he does so because he must; he has no choice except repression. The restriction of choice, of course, results from past experiences which taught him that he *must* repress.

To make a further analogy of repression of emotions, let us consider what would happen if one had to wear one's right arm in a sling, repressing its function. Within a comparatively short time the arm would become atrophied and useless, and after a while the entire body would suffer as a result of this restriction of function of one of its parts. So it is, I believe, with emotion: the restriction of this function will ultimately result in dysfunction of the entire organism.

In therapy, then, we try to assist the patient to express his own emotions. If he finds, during his recollections of a certain scene, that he feels angry, it is suggested that he express his anger in whatever manner seems appropriate.

(P.) . . . *and my father says, "Stop that! Don't ever do that again!"* (T.) *How does that make you feel?* (P.) *I feel annoyed—damn annoyed.* (T.) *If you could express*	Here is an event in which the patient has been restrained from expressing an emotion. The wisdom of this restraint or the justification for it is not germane to the therapy at this point—we are concerned only with the fact that here

this annoyance with your father how would you do it? What would you like to do?
(P.)   *I'd just push him away.*
(T.)   *All right, imagine that your father is in front of you —now push him away.*
(P.)   (*Makes gestures of pushing away repeatedly until he laughs.*) *I guess I'm not mad at him any more. I must have been a problem to him.*

is unexpressed emotion. The patient expresses one form of anger—rejection, forcible ejection. He might also have felt like hitting his father; in that case my technique is to suggest that he imagine his father's face on the couch where he can hit it with his fist, and ask him to pound the couch until I observe a change in the level of affect—usually 10 or 12 blows.

Occasionally the patient falsely identifies the target of his anger, and projects this emotion against the therapist. When this occurs, the same technique is used—the patient is asked to imagine hitting the therapist's face as if it were on the couch beside him. When the anger has been dissipated by expression, we have the patient look for the original target, the person with whom the therapist is temporarily identified.

If hitting the couch does not appear to give the patient a sufficient outlet for abreaction, I have him strike my hand as it lies on the couch at his side—a painless procedure, I can assure you. The reactions to this have sometimes been profound, and include expressions of love and copious weeping.

In the patient who has been exceedingly repressed, whose emotional expressiveness has atrophied into apathy, we sometimes observe that he is unable to express his emotions even in this substitute fashion. Our task, then, is to determine the source or sources of this repression and let him realize it. This is seldom easy; one method which is worth trying is to have him look for events in which he "exercised admirable self-control." By implying that emotional repression is admirable, we can get the patient to discuss it fully enough to give us a clue as to who taught him to repress emotions.

Another reason for repression is a confusion between emotions, such as is seen in the person who cries when he is angry or laughs when he is sad. Without attempting to put a value-judgment on which emotions "should" be expressed at any given time, I have observed that there are certain *appropriate* emotions, the appropriateness being determined on a consensual basis. They might be tabulated as follows:

Stimulus-pattern	"Appropriate" emotional response
Restriction of activity	Anger
Activities which, if continued, might lead to "Death."	Fear
Occurrences in which survival had been predicted but "Death" actually occurred.	Weeping
Occurrences in which "Death" had been predicted but survival actually occurred.	Laughter

When a patient substitutes one form of emotional expression for another, we are presented with the difficult task of finding the events which engendered such a confusion. One which I have found frequently is seen in the individual who cries whenever he becomes angry; as a concomitant of this confusion we usually see that he also becomes angry when he cries or when anyone else cries. This patient acts as if he is unable to cry, because that might make him angry, and is unable to become angry, because that might make him cry.

In our society our children are usually restrained from crying as much as possible. Boys, especially, are told not to cry, are told that only sissies cry, that "big boys don't cry," etc. How, then, could such a person become angry, if anger is equated with crying?

Resolution of such a confusion is carried out in two ways: one, we look for the events in which there were both anger and tears, and, two, we try to persuade the person to express one or the other of these emotions in an event wherein there was a minimum of confusion. In this chapter we shall confine ourselves to the discussion of searching for a relatively unmixed emotion.

The type of event in which grief is the paramount feeling is the death of a loved one. The death may be an actual one, or it may be a functional type of demise, where the object of the patient's affection is lost by separation. The patient, on a less-than-conscious level, acts as if his chances for survival were completely enmeshed with the other person's existence; he predicts, as it were, that if the other dies, he dies too. It is the therapist's task to persuade the patient to review the event in which death of a loved one (or "ally") occurred, and to realize that he himself did not actually die; in order to arrive at this realization, the patient must release the emotional tension which acts as a preservative of the false-to-fact association.

It should be noted, incidentally, that the ally does not have to be human or even animate. I have often observed grief, sincere and real, expressed at the loss of a dog or even a toy teddy-bear. It has, in some cases, seemed necessary to review losses of non-human allies before the patient can recall completely the losses of human allies.

The technique used to obtain a discharge of grief at the loss of an ally is as follows: first, in taking the history we inquire about the deaths which have occurred in the patient's family, and note the age of the patient at which the deaths occurred. We try to determine the degree of affection which the patient bore towards these people, and vice versa, keeping in mind that an especially casual attitude may be concealing a deep affection and identification.

We can often get a clue as to the person over whose loss hangs the deepest pall of grief by observing whether the patient rubs his eyes. The rubbing of the eyes seems to be an activity which, among other things, indicates the presence of tears and hence grief.

At some moment in therapy, usually after the patient has become accustomed to recalling the specific perceptual background in specific experiences, we ask him to return to the moment when the death of the ally occurred.

(T.) *Let's see what you can recall about the death of your mother. Where were you when she died?*

(P.) *In the hospital; I was right with her to the last.*

(T.) *Let's go to the hospital. Who else is there?*

(P.) *My brother and the doctor.*

(T.) *Can you see the doctor?*

(P.) *Yes; he's standing at the right side of the bed.*

(T.) *Where are you?*

(P.) *I'm standing at the left side, and my brother is standing at the foot of the bed.*

The therapist tries, as usual, to guide the patient to a complete perceptual recollection of the event. In this case it seems advisable to get the backgound sketched in before touching the climactic area of the death. It is advisable to locate the others in the scene because of the possibility of other emotions being directed at them; if so, it seems to confuse the emotional response of the patient.

(T.) *How does your mother look? Can you see her?*

(P.) *Oh, yes—she's thin and pale; she's been sick for a long time.*

(T.) *Try to recall how you feel.*

We might, in some cases, get a grief discharge at this point. The patient might suddenly stop talking, turn his head away and start to sob. If there is no indication that the patient is on the verge of tears, the therapist continues with his attempts to establish the scene.

(P.) *Oh—I'm sort of glad that it's the end.*

(T.) *What happens next?*

(P.) *The doctor puts a stethoscope on her chest.*

(T.) *What is the doctor wearing?*

(P.) *He's an interne—he has a white coat on.*

(T.) *Is there any smell in the room?*

(P.) *It smells like a hospital.*

(T.) *Try to imagine what a hospital smells like; can you get the odor?*

(P.) *I can smell it—ugh.*

(T.) *What does the doctor say?*

(P.) *He listens to her chest and says, "Well, she's gone."*

The patient's report of his feelings suggests that he is partially rationalizing. The therapist gets the patient to recall more of the details in order to pull the appropriate emotion into the picture. We find it quite useful to stress the perception of odor in any experience in a hospital; this sensation is characteristic and notably restimulating. Again, we might see the release of affect at this point. It is advisable to have the patient repeat the words, "Well, she's gone," a half-dozen times or so, observing his responses. If his actions indicate incipient weeping—such actions as retraction of the jaw, trembling of the chin, rubbing the eyes and slight nasal congestion—further repetition of the phrase might lead to tears. If, on the other hand, the patient appears more tense and acts as if he were restraining himself from crying, we look for the factors which are blocking his expression of grief.

(T.)   *How do you feel about this doctor?*
(P.)   *Oh, all right—this is all in a day's work for him, I guess.*
(T.)   *But how do you feel about him?*
(P.)   *Well, I'm sort of annoyed at him. He seems too matter-of-fact about it.*

The therapist is looking for an emotion which might be preferred; in other words, if he could become angry he wouldn't have to express grief. If the patient seems to be substituting one emotion for another, it is necessary to resolve the preferred emotion before the grief can be expressed. In this case the patient's annoyance (anger) about the callousness which he imputes to the doctor seems to act as a block to grief.

(T.)   *What would you like to do to the doctor right here?*
(P.)   *Nothing—he's doing his job.*

By this imaginary device, the patient's saying what he might have said, he seems to discharge an unexpressed

(T.) *What would you like to tell him?*

(P.) *I'd like to tell him to get out.*

(T.) *Imagine the doctor's face before you—tell him to get out.*

(P.) *(Repeats "get out" several times.)*

(T.) *Let's return to this scene again. Look at your mother; notice how she's breathing.*

(P.) *Yes—she's gasping. Huh.*

(T.) *What is it?*

(P.) *I was just thinking— my wife's breathing sounds like that when we have intercourse. Strange . . .*

(T.) *Listen to your mother breathe: what does the doctor say?*

(P.) *"Well, she's gone."*

emotion. We observe the patient closely during his repetition of this phrase, noticing if there is any change in his bodily position, whether his fists are clenched or not. If a few repetitions leads to some relaxation, we infer that the anger has evaporated; if the attitudes of anger persist, we look for anger directed at someone else—in this case, the patient's brother. Let us assume that the patient has discharged the anger in the scene.

Here is an example of the apparently inappropriate associations which patients sometimes make. Yet it is important, because such an association may act as a deterrent to complete enjoyment of marital relations. It is usually unnecessary to elaborate this association between death-sounds and coitus-sounds any further; the patient has recognized the false-to-fact relationship. It would be well to note this for possible further exploration

at another session, especially
if the patient has complained
of sexual difficulties.

When the patient begins to weep, we have him recount the
scene repeatedly until he no longer has the tendency to express his grief. The usual procedure is for the therapist to
say, "Let's go through this again . . . look at your mother
. . . notice how thin and pale she looks . . . listen to her
breathing . . . notice what the doctor is doing . . . notice
the odor in the room . . . listen to her take her last
breath . . . notice how this makes you feel . . . what
does the doctor say?" This repetition is continued, usually
eight or ten times, until the patient appears to be somewhat
bored with it. If the boredom does not become manifest, the
therapist looks for other bits of emotionally-charged content,
such as the sympathy of the nurse, or the lack of understanding of the brother.

In case that further review of the patient's mother's death
produces *no* sign of affect-discharge, the therapist considers
several possibilities. One, the patient might have wept unrestrainedly at the time of his mother's death, and there was
adequate relief from tension. Another explanation is that
there is another area of grief—and if such is the case, it is
usually more recent—which acts as if it were superimposed
on this event, blocking it. A third explanation is that the patient has been given numerous commands, painfully enforced,
not to cry. Still another possibility is that this is not the moment when he realized that his mother was dead. He might
have concluded she was dead when the doctor told him she
wasn't expected to live or, even more common, the scene at his
mother's death-bed might have had less emotional impact
than the scene of her funeral.

The therapist then chooses which of the possibilities to explore. My usual practice is to go to the scene of the funeral first and observe the patient's response. If he indicates that he would prefer *not* to recall that event, by all means see that he does so.

One device which seems to free a patient from the bonds of emotional inexpressivity is to ask him to imagine what he would say to the departed loved one. We often note that there is an urge to express thanks for what has been done, or to tell of his love. I recall one patient whose emotional repression was so severe that I almost despaired of his seemingly lost abilities to express his feelings; when I asked him to visualize the appearance of his mother in her coffin and to tell her that he loved her, he was finally able to discharge the grief which he had carried within himself for years. He made the remark that he was always ashamed to tell her such things—a fine example of a psychically warped, though socially acceptable, behavior pattern.

We have considered both anger and grief and their expressions, which brings us to the third emotion which can restrict both therapy and day-to-day living. It was mentioned before that a part of the mind seems to work as a predictor mechanism. It takes the data which have been acquired in previous experiences, compares them with the percepts at hand and decides what action to take to secure the maximum pleasure and the minimum threat to survival. It appears as if fear results when the predicted outcome is death or any state which is equi-significant with death. For example, "heaven," "hell," "damned," and "all through" have been reactively interpreted by patients as being death threats.

It is obvious that the possibility of impending death can call forth the emotion of fear. What is not so obvious is that these equivalents of death appear to be as terrifying to the patient as death itself, and it frequently requires considerable insight and skill to recognize them. To cite an example, in both death and in therapy a person lies down with his eyes closed; these similarities seem to be sufficient to make some patients quite fearful of the therapy process. Another example is seen in the patient who has learned that people often appear to get better just before they die. "Getting better" to this patient is, therefore, the equivalent of impending death, on the reactive level of mental function, and he may be expected to resist any therapeutic measure which might threaten him with improvement.

It is my practice to inquire frequently of my patients, "What would happen to you if you did?" whenever the patient says, "I can't remember," or "I don't get anything," or some similar statement of inability to act. Often the answer is, "Nothing." To that I ask, "What would you say about a person to whom nothing happens?" The answer to that, of course, is, "He's dead." Still another answer to the question, "What would happen to you if you got better?" is the apparently jocose retort, "I wouldn't know." If the therapist considers this as a literal answer to his question—and we find that it is advisable to consider all answers in such a manner— he sees that "getting better" is equated with losing one's ability to know and hence is dangerous. It might appear to be belaboring a point of interpretation in considering seemingly casual replies as indications of danger, I admit; yet it seems to be therapeutically beneficial to help the patient recognize that he might be seeing a threat of death in every activity.

There is an interesting corollary to this concept of fear as a reaction toward all activities which are reactively equated with death—it enables us to deal with the phenomenon which the psychoanalysts call "resistance" in a more operational manner. With the viewpoint that "resistance" is the effort of the patient to avoid situations which to him signify death, instead of a form of conflict with the therapist, we are better able to search for the events which caused him to make that significance-equation.

I have as yet been unable to find any way in which a patient can express terror or fear in order to be freed from the tension which accompanies it. With anger, we can have the patient pound the couch where he imagines his antagonist's face to be; with grief, the patient seems to be freed from tension by crying. When we suggest that the patient assume an attitude or perform an action which would demonstrate his terror, we have observed that he gets into the foetal position or that he says he would "just like to shrink up." This might, incidentally, be regarded as suggestive evidence of the existence of prenatal "memory," although, of course, there are many other possible explanations.

At present we are considering the idea that anger and fear are the two extremes of a single state; anger might be described as epinephrine + aggressive action, fear as epinephrine + the action of fleeing. If such is the case, perhaps expression of rage may be a way to release fear. As yet there have been too few observations for me to do more than mention the idea.

In therapy, the only way I know of to resolve fear is to have the patient re-experience the phobogenic event and to integrate his recollections of it with his conscious memories, re-evaluating it in the light of his total knowledge. The reassurance afforded by permissive positive suggestions, such as "You don't have to be afraid if you don't want to," seem to augment the patient's abilities to face these terrifying recollections and associations.

Fear, either in the therapy situation or in everyday life situations, is seldom manifested as overt terror. Much more commonly seen is anxiety, with its concomitant manifestations of rapid heart rate, labile blood-pressure, cold, moist hands, and an easily-elicited startle reaction. It is my impression that anxiety results when the patient has only a limited number of choices of action, all of which give rise to predicted death or its equivalent. The patient literally does not know which way to turn, and he vacillates from one possible solution to another with his emotional tension constantly mounting until a change in his environment offers an avenue of escape. If no way of escape becomes manifest, the patient is apt to develop a fear paralysis—the so-called "opossum reaction." We can often help such a patient merely by pointing out that he has other alternatives for reaction than the ones which he predicts as ultimately fatal.

The mixed emotion called "shame" has, in my opinion, an element of fear in it. I have often seen a shame reaction occur when a person has done to someone else what has already been done to him; the patient was hurt; he hurts someone else in a similar fashion, and he feels ashamed of his deed. The fear seems to be associated with the re-enactment as well as the possibility of retaliation.

A discussion of emotion would not be complete without some mention of the physical sensations which accompany the various emotional states. For example, we have observed previously that many patients will rub their eyes when they approach any events in which there is the emotion of grief. There is frequently a report of a cold sensation in the abdomen or in the epigastrium as a concomitant of fear, and the patient is seen to become generally tense. Anger seems to produce an increase in tonus of the masseter muscles—almost as if the patient were preparing to take a bite out of his antagonist.

Observation of the patient will reveal these attitudinal signs, and we can make use of them in therapy. Their greatest applicability is in the patient who acts as if he must deny the existence of his emotions. We ask, "How do you feel?" and the patient answers, "Just fine" or "All right." If we notice that the patient has a clenched fist and tense jaw muscles, we can suspect that he is somatically angry in spite of being semantically "all right."

We can use this observation in two ways: one, we can call the attention of the patient to his attitude and ask him for the possible significance of it, thereby making him aware that at least part of him is angry and that his actions are belying his words. Secondly, we can ask the patient to review the times in his life when he had clenched fists and a tense jaw and endeavor to permit him to re-experience an emotion.

There is one more phenomenon which tends to make a case "difficult" that is worthy of mention—somnolence. Most patients will, at some point in their therapy, be seen to become extremely sleepy during a session; the sleepiness may be of such depth that it is difficult to arouse them. The causes for this somnolence seem to be: one, a redramatization of deep unconsciousness; two, the obedience to a command within the situation being reviewed which says, in effect, "Go to sleep"; thirdly, it may be a behavior-pattern of the patient which enables him to evade unpleasant, painful situations such as might be encountered in therapy.

We can use several different methods to bring the patient out of his somnolence and back into a state where he is better able to cooperate with the therapist. One method is to ask the patient to interpret the words which he has already ascribed to the event which he is reviewing; the intellectual exercise of becoming aware of the multiordinality of meaning seems to relieve the somnolence. Second, we can ask the patient if somebody might have said something like "Go to sleep" in this incident; if so, repetition of the command will bring him to a state of wakefulness.

Another device is to say, "Let's assume that there is a period of time in this event where you were unconscious, and let's go through that period of unconsciousness on the count of five. At 'one' you will go to the moment when the unconsciousness begins; at 'five' you will be at the point where you are fully conscious again. All right?" When the patient assents to this, the therapist counts, "One . . . two . . . three . . . four . . . five. . . ." slowly and repeatedly. After every six countings-through or so, the therapist asks, "What seems to be happening?" or "Do any other words occur to you?" or "What are you thinking about?" If the patient reports a dream, he may be asked to interpret it and is thereby awakened. If he brings up new words, he is asked to repeat them. If he reports any sensation, he is asked to become aware of it and to tell of his associations with it.

The effects of this counting technique are somewhat variable and unpredictable; it is a device which is not used frequently. I mention it merely to indicate that such a method has been employed, with the suggestion that it might warrant a more extensive study.

In dealing with the somnolent patient, permissive suggestion can also be used, such as "You can wake up if you want to—you don't have to go to sleep."

If these methods seem to be ineffectual, the patient can be asked to wake up and become aware of his present surroundings; the reasons for his sleepiness and possible explanations can then be discussed with the patient in the awake state for a few moments before sending him back to the incident in which he became somnolent.

Ultimately the patient will begin to yawn and stretch; when he does this the somnolence seems to disappear.

One should not confuse the somnolence seen during therapy with the sleepiness which occasionally affects the patient after the session. The latter condition is frequently the relaxation resulting from therapeutic release of tension; we also find that yawning during a session seems to be an adequate stimulus for post-session drowsiness; it may not necessarily have any therapeutic significance.

PRECAUTIONS IN THERAPY

——— VI ———

Every practitioner of any art or skill must learn that there are certain precautionary measures to be taken. The carpenter learns that he can't put his finger against a rotating circular saw and expect to get off unscathed. The automobile driver learns that he can't pass another car on a hill without an increased probability of injury. The anesthetist learns that his patient must get oxygen as well as the anesthetic.

In the instruction of a neophyte, there is a strong tendency for the teacher to make emphatic and didactic statements about the things which the student should *not* do. As often as not, the student goes ahead and does them, with results which might be tragic or comic.

In this book I shall try to avoid setting up an iron-clad list of the Do's and Don'ts. Permit me, instead, to tell of the things which I do not do, and the experiences I have had which led me to those conclusions.

I make a special effort not to evaluate anything which my patients say, and any evaluation which I might make I do *not* discuss with the patient. Whatever a patient says during therapy, I accept as a statement—nothing more. If a patient asks, at the end of a session, "Well, do you think we got any place today?" my answer is, "What do you think?" If a patient says during therapy. "Oh, this isn't real *—it couldn't have happened," my answer is, "You know whether it's real or not—but let's investigate it anyway." If a patient says, "This seems awfully real; it must have happened," my answer is, "Is that so? Tell me about it some more." And if a patient absolutely insists on my evaluating some event which he has recalled, I can always use the phrase, "Very interesting."

My reasons for avoiding evaluations are many. I feel that it is the task of the patient to make *his own* evaluations; his aberrated conduct is, to a large extent, the result of evaluations made by others, and it is only as he shifts to new and personal evaluations that therapy takes place. The person who feels that he is "no damn good" has that feeling because someone told him so, and enforced that evaluation with pain. If a girl acts as if every man were a menace to her life, it might be because she has had at least one experience wherein "man" was equated with "death"—an evaluation which she was constrained to make by the force of circumstances within a specific event or events.

It is possible to speak of the aim in therapy in many different ways; we might say that therapy is a process wherein patients learn to realize that they can evaluate each situation on the basis of *all* their past experiences. Perhaps the patient was

---

*The therapist, incidentally, should not be misled by the patient's denial of the reality of an incident. It seems that a patient goes inevitably to something which is bothering him and that the incident he reviews, no matter how fantastic, contains a portion of reality. The skilled therapist will attempt to find out why the patient brought up this incident in the first place.

told that he was "no damn good"—but he was also told that he was "cute," "smart," "stupid," "intellectual," etc. Perhaps a girl was injured at one time by a man—but that doesn't necessarily mean that every man is a threat to her life. People *can* differentiate—and differentiation, along with evaluation, goes hand in hand with survival.

Every person has, by the time he reaches maturity, a vast store of data. When any situation presents itself, he can compare this data from the present with his recorded data from the past; he can, I believe, recognize that he has numerous alternatives for action. He has enough data to evaluate these alternatives and to choose a course of action which has the highest possible survival value. This, as I see it, is the innate function of the mind.

We find that the experiences in which a person was not permitted or was not able to make a choice are the ones which lead to neurosis and mental malfunction. Why, then, should I attempt to confuse a patient further by making an evaluation for him? It is *his* choice.

I consider interpretation as a corollary of evaluation, and I therefore refrain from interpreting a patient's recollections. If I ask a patient to return to the first time he had a certain symptom, I do not specify or decide for him when that first time was. If he says that his impression of his surroundings includes darkness, warmth, moisture and a floating sensation, I do not try to persuade him that he is "prenatal." I might, however, ask him as to his interpretation. If the patient chooses to interpret these sensations as indicating a recollection of intra-uterine life, I accept it; if, on the contrary, he chooses to identify the scene as one when he was taking a bath and the lights went out, I accept that.

It should be pointed out that patients should be given the opportunity of considering "prenatal" recollections; to deny that one might have such recollections would in itself be an interference with the patient's evaluations. I must confess that my rather tentative acceptance of this concept leads me to present it as an assumption, rather than a certainty.

To allow a patient to consider a group of associated perceptions as "prenatal" in origin, I use this gambit: "Do you suppose that these sensations of darkness, warmth and moisture might appear during prenatal life?" "Would you have any objection to considering that there might be such a thing as prenatal awareness?" "Would you like to see if you could re-experience a prenatal event?" "Suppose, for the purposes of further discussion, that the unborn infant could know what its mother is saying; what do you suppose that your mother would have said under these circumstances?"

Most patients, I notice, when approached this way will utilize the possibility of prenatal "memory," at least for the purpose of further discussion. Clinical observation leads me to conclude that therapeutic benefits can be obtained from having them consider such possibilities, especially when the patient is not required to believe that such a possibility is a probability or a certainty.

In other words, the therapist should feel as if he can offer possibilities for the consideration of the patient, but he should not, I believe, require that the patient accept the therapist's possibility as his own fact. Patients who have been forced to conform to the mores of their group or their families are apt to accede to the therapist's suggestions all too willingly, and one should be cautious not to confuse docility with therapy.

As an example of this, there is the case of the female patient who had been punished frequently by her parents for minor infractions of family rules. She had developed into a person who was propitiative, eager to please and amenable to suggestion. Along with this went a severe anxiety, which at times bordered on stark terror. She was given dianetic therapy by an "auditor" who preferred the forceful approach, and who would push her into recalling a scene, rather than telling her that she was able to get into it. During one session she recalled a very painful event in her past and became terrified, asking, "Do I have to go through with this?" The "auditor" told her forcefully, "You have no choice; you *must* go through with it."

Shortly after this session the patient developed a noticeable abulia. She was extremely indecisive about numerous commonplace activities. She would stand at a street-crossing, unable to decide whether to walk across or to wait; finally she would force herself to cross. It was as if she were obeying, implicitly and literally, the commands, "You have no choice," and "You must go through with it."

A few weeks later she had a session with another therapist, and she recalled and reviewed the previous session. The indecisiveness abated promptly and the concomitant anxiety disappeared.

My understanding of this situation is that she was given a positive suggestion in the hypnotic sense by the first auditor, and it appeared as if the therapeutic benefits obtained from the first session were partially nullified by the implantation of a statement which restricted her ability to choose.

Had I been the therapist at the first session, my technique would have been to ask, "What do you suppose might happen if you went through with this? You lived through it once; don't you suppose that you could live through it again? What would happen to you if you didn't go through with it? Which would you rather do—feel a little pain now and find out about it or run away from this incident?" My efforts, in other words, would be aimed at increasing the patient's ability to decide that therapy was preferable to evasion. If I thought it necessary, I might also have said, "You *can* go through with this, if you want to. You have the courage to face it."

Note, if you please, the difference between saying, "You must!" and "You can." The first is a restrictive positive suggestion, allowing the patient no choice, and usually restimulating the original authoritarian pressure from which the patient's difficulties are derived in the first place. The second is permissive, allowing the patient to choose whatever alternative he wishes. I firmly believe that permissive positive suggestions which enlarge the scope of available alternatives are always therapeutically permissible and usually therapeutically beneficial.

When it is necessary for the therapist to offer the patient a choice, he might do it in this manner:

(T.)   What sensation do you have now?

(P.)   My eyes feel as if I want to rub them.

(T.)   What do you suppose could cause that feeling?

(P.)   Having something in my eye—a cinder maybe.

(T.)   Anything else?

(P.)   Having "pink eye."

(T.)   Anything else?

(P.)   I can't think of anything.

(T.)   There are some possibilities I can think of; you don't have to accept them, of course. Could your eyes feel like this if you were crying?

(P.)   Yes, I guess so.

(T.)   Could your eyes feel like this if someone put drops in them?

(P.)   Certainly.

(T.)   All right, let's try to recall the first time your eyes felt this way.

There is another aspect of evaluation which should not be overlooked—the authoritarian aspect. Those of us who have closely observed dianetic therapy and have compared it with other psychotherapies have noted an inverse correlation between the degree of authoritarianism and the amount of therapeutic benefit obtained by the patient. A system of thought which says, in essence, "This is *the* way, the only way, to think," soon leads its adherents into a condition of rigidity and stasis.

In our present-day society, the tendency towards authoritarianism is noteworthy; examples can be seen in forms of government, in educational systems, in religions. Even our advertising has its appeals based on what "doctors say" or "science has proved" or "men of distinction prefer." It therefore seems justifiable to stress, in therapy, the antithetical view and to restore to our patients the awareness of their abilities to choose between conformism and non-conformism.

Occasionally we shall find among our patients individuals who are extreme non-conformists—so extreme in their negativism that they are essentially as reactionary as those against whom they are negating. With them we must be doubly careful not to evaluate, either pro or contra, for in so doing we might produce a reaction against therapy. As an example of this, there was the patient who had the phrase, "Even if it was true, I wouldn't believe it," as part of the verbal content of several traumatic experiences. A therapist once made the mistake of saying that he thought that this patient's recollections sounded valid to him—and, because of this belief-negating command, the patient temporarily acted as if he denied all the beneficial sessions which he had previously had.

But enough of this discussion of evaluation; suffice it to say that I have found it most inadvisable. You may choose to differ with me—if so, I shall not attempt to evaluate your opinions.

There is another important consideration in the therapy session: the reduction of discomfort. My practice is to spare no effort to make certain that the patient is comfortable by the end of the session.

When a patient has returned to a painful incident, he will to some degree re-experience the pain; he may not be aware of the pain or may be unable, apparently, to clarify his perception of the pain during the session, but it is my impression that the pain is there, nonetheless. The pain can be exhausted by repetition in the majority of cases. If it is not, the patient at the end of the session experiences the pain in "present time," where it is much more obvious and disturbing.

I have observed, as an example of this, that when a patient is asked to return to birth, he soon develops a headache. The pressure on and the molding of the neonatal head, as observed during an obstetrical delivery, makes such a reaction highly probable. During the time the patient is "in birth" while on the couch, the pain is quite tolerable. If, however, the patient is made abruptly aware of his present surroundings, the headache becomes extremely intense and the patient is subjected to needless misery. Moreover, the other conditions of the body which are present in birth can be re-activated, and we may observe that the patient has a stuffed-up nose, or inflammation of the eyes, or respiratory difficulties, or abdominal pain; his resistance to respiratory infection seems to be lowered, and the common cold is a frequent aftermath of a session wherein birth is touched and the pain not reduced.

Reduction of pain can usually be obtained by repetition, especially if the therapist concentrates on a small segment of the time of birth. An example follows:

The patient has been asked to return to birth; he has reported a headache and a stuffy nose, and the therapist observes that he changes his position frequently on the couch.

(T.)   What else do you suppose that you'd feel?

(P.)   I don't know. Say, I can't take this much longer.

(T.)   Do you suppose that someone might have used the phrase, "Take this," during your birth?

(P.)   Yes, I suppose that the doctor might have said it.

(T.)   What might he be doing at the time?

(P.)   I guess that he'd be handing me over to the nurse.

(T.)   And what would the doctor be saying?

(P.)   "Here, you can take this now." No, that doesn't seem quite right.

(T.)   Change the words to suit yourself.

(P.)   "Here, you can take *him* now." That's it.

(T.)   Repeat the phrase, please, and notice how your head feels.

(P.)   (Repeats phrase 5 or 6 times.)

(T.)   Notice how your nose feels as you go over these words. Repeat them again.

(P.)   (More repetitions.)

(T.)   How's the headache now?

(P.)   It's getting worse. (Rubs his eyes.)

(T.)   How about your eyes—what sensation do you suppose they'd have?

(P.)   They're stinging; it must be those damn drops he put in.

(T.)   How do you feel about the doctor putting drops in your eyes?

(P.)   I'm mad at him; that's a dirty trick.

(T.)   Supposing that you could get even with the doctor; what would you like to do to him?

(P.)   I'd like to hit him. (Words are spoken in a resentful tone.)

(T.)   All right—imagine that the doctor's face is on the couch beside you. Now hit it!

(P.)   (Clenches jaws and strikes at the couch with closed fist; makes about ten blows.)

(T.)   Go ahead—get good and mad at him. Hit him again!

(P.)   (Laughs.) I can't—it's too silly.

(T.)   How's the headache now?

(P.)   Better.

(T.)   Now let's put all these associations together in a pattern. Notice your headache . . . notice how your eyes feel . . . your nose . . . the feeling of anger. Anything else?

(P.)   (Scratches at ribs along left axillary line) Funny— I was just thinking about the way my sister used to tickle me. I haven't thought about that in years.

(T.)   What sensation might you have had in birth that would remind you of being tickled?

(P.)   I don't know. (Scratches chest again.)

(T.)   How do you suppose that the doctor picked you up?

(P.)   He could have picked me up with his hand under my chest there.

(T.)   Imagine how it would feel to have someone pick you up. What would the temperature of his hand be?

(P.)   Warm, I guess.

(T.)   And what does he say?

(P.)   "Here, you can take him now."

(T.)   Where is "now"?

(P.)   Why, *now*—present time.

(T.)   Are you being born in 1951?

(P.)   No—of course not.

(T.)   You can differentiate between "now," if it was said at the time of your birth, and "now" in 1951, can't you?

(P.)   Sure.

(T.)   Supposing that your headache obeyed the command, "Take him now." What might happen?

(P.)   I don't know—I can't seem to figure that one out.

(T.)   What does "take" mean?

(P.)   It means to carry . . . to steal . . . to grasp . . . to attract.

(T.)   And where is now?

(P.)   Oh, I see—that could mean that my headache would be taken to present time.

(T.)   Do you have to bring your birth-headache up to present time just because the doctor said, "Take him now"?

(P.)   No. That's silly.

(T.)   How's the headache now?

(P.)   Much better—practically gone.

As can be seen, the method of reducing pain is somewhat different from the techniques previously discussed. The method can be explained by an analogy: consider a field of experience with the dimensions of the body at birth extending through the duration of the phrase, "Take him now." Within the limits of this temporo-spatial experience are numerous perceptic recordings—but the patient has focussed his awareness only on one: the headache. By redirecting his attention to other parts of the field, making him aware of the synchronic associations, the pain of the headache is diffused and thereby eliminated. It is therefore desirable that the therapist be familiar with all the possibilities for sensation in birth so that he can explore as many of them as necessary to secure the patient's comfort.

It has been observed that this modification of technique seems to secure satisfactory reduction of pain with a minimum of post-session discomfort; it is recommended for use when a restimulated pain persists stubbornly.

An analysis of this technique follows:

(T.) *What else do you suppose that you'd feel?*
(P.) *I don't know. Say, I can't take this much longer.*

The therapist suspects the phrase, "Take this," because of the restrictive choice-denying implication. It could be, of course, that the patient was only complaining about the intensity of his headache, but the phrase is of a type which bears investigation.

(T.) *Do you suppose that someone might have used the phrase "take this" during your birth?*
(P.) *Yes, I suppose that the doctor might have said it.*

The patient chooses to attribute this to the doctor. It might be equally possible that the mother used this idiom as a complaint of the unbearability of her pain. In any case, the therapist is looking for a point in birth containing this phrase in order to concentrate upon it.

(T.) *What might he be doing at the time?*

(P.) *I guess that he'd be handing me over to the nurse.*

(T.) *And what would he be saying?*

(P.) *"Here, you can take this now." That doesn't seem quite right.*

(T.) *Change the words to suit yourself.*

(P.) *"Here, you can take him now." That's it.*

The therapist, in using the words "might" and "suppose," is giving the patient the opportunity to choose an acceptable probability. We note that the patient puts his own evaluation on the acceptability of his first attempt to form a phrase. The therapist gives him a permissive suggestion, and the patient chooses to alter the phrase. The action of the doctor which accompanies the words is noted for later use.

(P.) *(Repeats.)*

(T.) *Notice how your nose feels.*

(P.) *(Repeats.)*

(T.) *How's the headache now?*

(P.) *It's getting worse. (Rubs his eyes.)*

(T.) *How about your eyes —what sensation do you suppose they'd have?*

(P.) *They're stinging; it must be those damn drops he put in.*

(T.) *How do you feel about the doctor putting drops in your eyes?*

The therapist is trying to broaden the patient's focus of awareness, helping him to "get into the incident" further. The increase in severity of the headache indicates that this is being accomplished. The rubbing of the eyes indicates that "here is a time-place where the eyes feel as if they should be rubbed." The use of the adjective "damn" indicates an emotional reaction towards the act of putting in drops; the therapist inquires about the reaction as it might be directed towards the author of the discomfort.

(P.) *I'm mad at him; that's a dirty trick.*
(T.) *Supposing that you could get even with the doctor; what would you like to do to him?*
(P.) *I'd like to hit him.*
(T.) *Imagine that the doctor's face is on the couch beside you. Now hit it!*
(P.) *(Strikes at the couch with closed fist. . . .)*
(T.) *Go ahead—get good and mad at him. Hit him again!*
(P.) *(Laughs.) I can't— it's too silly.*
(T.) *How's the headache now?*
(P.) *Better.*

The patient demonstrates here an interesting and characteristic mood—the anger and resentment which appear to be an almost invariable concomitant of birth. It is my belief that this rage, which at the time was only partially expressed, is an important factor in making birth a traumatic and aberrative experience. It is demonstrated to the patient that he *can* release this anger by taking a physical action. The therapist, by using vernacular and idiomatic language, emphasizes the unsophistication of the response. The laughter indicates that the emotional tension has been dissipated, and the intensity of the headache decreases simultaneously.

(T.) *Let's put all these associations together . . . etc. Anything else?*

The therapist directs the attention of the patient to the *pattern*, the integrated totality of sensation, mood and evaluation in this specific experience; he is concerned with the patient's sensations, moods and evaluations, making no attempt to decide whether or not this possible event actually occurred.

(P.) (*Scratches . . .*) *Funny, I was just thinking about the way my sister used to tickle me. I haven't thought about that in years.*

Note how the patient responds with an action-requiring sensation, rather than one on a verbal level. Note also that he makes an association between an early and a later tactile memory—an example of the stimulation of the memory process through increasing awareness. We also observe that head-scratching frequently accompanies memory contact with birth.

(T.) *How do you suppose the doctor picked you up?*
(P.) *He could have picked me up with his hand under my chest there.*
(T.) *Imagine how it would feel to have someone pick you up. What would the temperature of his hand be?*
(P.) *Warm, I guess.*

The therapist here is making a deductive short-cut which is usually justifiable. It is obvious that the baby was picked up at some point during delivery; the sensation to which the patient refers is most likely to be due to being picked up—ergo, the question is asked in this manner. Experience shows that if the patient were not ready to consider how he was picked up, he would express objections to the question.

This also brings up the point, only inferentially demonstrated in this example, that neonatal tactile sensations are highly important. The new-born, just out of his prenatal environment, where he floats in amniotic fluid, seems peculiarly aware of his first skin sensations—judging, of course, by the sort of evidence we get in our type of psychotherapy.

It should also be mentioned here that, no matter what the question is, the patient seems to bring up only the material which is troubling him; in a recollection of birth, as discussed here, each patient will give a different answer to the same question, and each answer seems to be a phase of the patient's individual problem. This, I feel, is in a sense evidence of the personal authenticity of the material.

(T.) *And what does he say?*

(P.) *"Here, you can take him now."*

(T.) *Where is "now"?*

(P.) *Why,* now—*present time.*

(T.) *Are you being born in 1951?*

(P.) *No—of course not.*

(T.) *You can differentiate between "now," if it was said at the time of your birth, and "now" in 1951, can't you?*

(P.) *Sure.*

The therapist encourages the patient to interpret possible meanings of the words which he has brought up. Illustrated here is an example of the confusion which results from using a word which is not anchored in Time. The timelessness of such a word as "now" seems to make the time of birth indistinguishable from time (1951) on the reactive level of the mind. The therapist points up the necessity for differentiation and the patient's ability to perform this function.

This particular example was chosen because the patient seemed to be well aware of the multiordinality of meanings of words. Not all patients have such a good grasp of this concept of the possible effect of words, literally interpreted, on a person's behavior pattern. I feel that it is important to encourage my patients to exercise their abilities to differentiate, although I have seen cases which were apparently benefited without as much stress placed on interpretation—or, as Hubbard calls it, "computation."

(T.) *Supposing that your headache obeyed the command, "Take him now." What might happen?*
(P.) *I don't know—I can't seem to figure that one out.*
(T.) *What does "take" mean?*
(P.) *It means to carry . . . steal . . . grasp . . . attract.*
(T.) *And where is now?*

This possibility was stressed with this patient because of the history of frequent headaches. The particular command might not have been a factor in his headaches, yet the therapist had to consider the possibility and have the patient evaluate it. It is noteworthy that the headache finally disap-

(P.) *Oh, I see—that could mean that my headache would be taken to present time.*

(T.) *Do you have to bring your birth headache up to present time just because the doctor said, "Take him now"?*

peared in this session when the patient's attention was directed towards this possible command-response.

This particular technique of taking one small segment of an experience and completely examining all possible associations has been the most effectual in producing complete abolition of discomfort during therapy. If this does not prove effectual, my practice is to look for a later event with similar discomfort or similar word-content, in which there is also some strong emotional state. Another method is to send the patient to an earlier event, assuming that there is a "prenatal" event which the patient can recall. Still another technique is to bring the patient to some recent event of pleasure unmarred by discomfort and have him re-experience it perceptually as fully as possible.

Let me emphasize again the urgent advisability of doing one's utmost to reduce all pain before terminating a session. One of my friends once, in discussing this subject, referred to therapy as "controlled insanity"; during the session the patient was living in a world not of the present time, acting in a manner incongruent with present-time reality, "hearing voices," responding to non-contemporaneous stimuli, etc.— behavior which was, in a sense, psychotic. I feel that this idea overemphasizes the potential dangers of therapy—but it might be considered as another reason for insisting on the practice of reducing all discomfort.

The concept of "controlled insanity" as a description of the therapy process is applicable not only to dianetics but to other psychotherapies as well. The control of the "insanity" is better, I feel, in dianetic therapy than it is in other therapies, especially those in which the patient is narcotized or hypnotized. The dianetic patient is always permitted to maintain contact with his present-time environment; he is assisted to become aware that he is dealing with perceptions and sensations which originated at a time other than that of the therapy session. The patient's awareness of present time is testified to by the ease with which he can be disturbed by such interruptions as the telephone bell ringing or sudden sounds outside of the therapy room; he is generally even aware of the therapist's lighting a cigarette.

In addition to the precautions which I have already discussed, I try to avoid making predictions. Patients will frequently ask for a prognosis in such a way that it seems as if they are asking for a guarantee: "Do you think I'll get over this? How long is it going to take?" Such questions need to be answered, and the words, "I don't know," are not, in my opinion, a satisfactory reply, in spite of their accuracy. I find it is better to say, "I am sure that you *can* get better. Whether or not you *will* is up to you. I'll do everything I can to help, but it is as much your responsibility as it is mine. And as to the length of therapy, that's up to you, too. Whenever you feel that you have had as much as you want, you're free to discontinue."

By this sort of reply I try to give the patient the permissive suggestion that he can choose to live a more effectual life, at the same time implying that it is *his* choice, not the therapist's. The patient is informed that his role in therapy is an active one; he is not going to lie down passively and be "cured" without efforts on his part.

Some patients find this attitude disturbing; they have been so subjected to authoritarianism that freedom of choice is unwelcome. But if the therapist makes a prediction which does not come true, the patient might construe this as evidence that the doctor was lying, and a relapse into anger or apathy can be expected.

It is obvious also that the therapist should not set up contingencies, such as, "If you don't get better, you won't have to pay me," or "If this doesn't work, we can try something else." Remember that the behavior-pattern which brings the patient to you has some survival-value; the patient's continuing existence, unhappy though it might be, gives evidence of its effectuality. Consequently, he is not going to give up this pattern for a still nebulous alternative if he is offered a loophole through which he can evade finding out about himself.

One final word of caution: in this sort of therapy we are dealing with the emergency reactions of the mind. They are quick, "unthinking" responses to situations which, in the light of past experience, offer a threat to survival. One should therefore encourage the patient to give quick, first-impression responses without attempt to evaluate or censor them. Countless hours of therapy time can be wasted if one permits a patient to rationalize and explain his conduct, to delay his answers until he has thought out some good sonorous phrases in which to express his thought. Delayed responses are good evidence of what one *thinks* he should think; we are looking for what he *does* think.

THERAPEUTIC BENEFITS

THERE HAVE BEEN numerous mentions of "therapeutic benefits" up to this point without any elaboration of what is meant by this term. It now seems appropriate to set forth a more specific exposition of the aims and the results of the therapeutic process.

In any therapy the first desire of the therapist is to halt the morbid process, to prevent it from getting worse. It is as if every illness contained a threat of death—as if the diseased person were saying to himself, "If I get any more sick, I'm going to die." It is commonly observed that this fact alone seems to be capable of perpetuating the illness.

The second desideratum in therapy is to obtain relief from the discomfort which accompanies illness. In any illness the pain itself seems to be an element which makes the illness more frightening and prevents the sufferer from continuing with his usual behavior pattern. In numerous pathologic conditions it is merely sufficient to relieve the patient of his pain to insure recovery.

A third task which any therapist tries to accomplish—though he might not be aware that he is doing so—is the prevention of over-compensation for an illness. This observation is prompted by Selye's work on the general adaptation syndrome, wherein he points out that death seems to be caused by the body's persistent attempts to compensate for a noxious stimulus long after there is any apparent necessity for the compensation process. To give a more commonly observed example, the phenomenon of fever seems to be a means of combatting certain infectious diseases; so long as the body temperature is elevated to a certain point the patient seems to benefit by it. But if the temperature becomes elevated beyond this point, the patient seems to be as much harmed by the hyperpyrexia as he is by the disease itself, and efforts are thereupon necessary to reduce the fever with antipyretics, tepid sponge-baths and so on.

The fourth effort of the therapist is to restore to the patient his former ability to function, to rehabilitate him on as high a level as possible. In so doing he tries to make the patient independent of further assistance and to make him at least as self-sustaining as he was before his illness supervened.

In evaluating therapeutic benefits, our group has these four categories in mind. Up until now, our judgments have been based on observations of our patients and on the reports which our patients give us. We are aware of the necessity for ultimately obtaining measurements of change, but we have refrained from embarking on any program of psychometry and/or clinical laboratory procedures until we are certain of just what changes we should measure. It should be obvious that a program of mensuration is difficult for a small, self-supporting group; one of the purposes of this book is to stimulate some such program of investigation by other groups better equipped to do this type of work.

Our analysis of therapeutic benefits has, therefore, been based almost entirely on clinical impressions. We have made a sufficient number of observations to be able to determine a strong trend, the various aspects of which can be listed as follows:

1. We observe that our patients act as if they were more aware of available alternatives of action. When presented with a problem, there is an attempt to solve the problem, rather than to evade the responsibility of solution in apathy or illness. An example of this is furnished by the patient who was suicidal at the start of therapy; at that time he could see no other solution to his difficulties but self-destruction. After a few weeks of therapy he decided that it would be better for him to start a new business, the decision being made on his own choice without prompting by the therapist.

2. We see fewer examples of inconclusive thinking. One patient, a female homosexual, had a highly ambivalent attitude toward her inamorata—she wanted to see her, yet she also wanted to terminate the affair, which she said was "vulgar and disgusting." After a few hours of therapy she was able to resolve this dilemma and broke off her friendship with the girl without whom she formerly "couldn't live."

3. There is a diminution of anxiety and a lessening of fear reactions. A patient with migraine, previous to therapy, would retire to his bed whenever he felt an attack coming on; he explained this behavior by saying, "I just know it will get worse if I stay up, and I don't want to take any chances of that happening." During therapy he seemed to develop a tolerance towards discomfort and would continue with his work despite the presence of a headache. Instead of being afraid of getting a headache, he would become annoyed at getting one; an attack of migraine became a period of lowered efficiency rather than one of complete immobilization.

4. Some of our patients have learned that there is no necessity for suffering pain. During therapy they are trained to increase or decrease the intensity of any "remembered" pain at will; they seem to be able to utilize this training pattern outside of therapy. A patient with chronic cervico-occipital myalgia has learned that whenever she has an attack of neck pain she can diminish it by alternately tensing and relaxing the muscles of her neck and back; during this exercise she focuses her awareness on her activities, and she reports that she is thus able to reduce her discomfort to a tolerable level. A similar acquisition of control has been reported by a patient with exophthalmos—by deliberately "popping" her eyes, observing this in a mirror, she is able to decrease the amount of protrusion of her eyeballs whenever they become prominent.

It seems, moreover, that the knowledge that pain can be relieved by a psychotherapeutic process without resort to medication acts to make it less important and less productive of anxiety.

5. There seems to be less of a tendency for a patient to get into a diminishing spiral of illness and an enhanced ability to get out of such a spiral without exterior aid. An alcoholic patient before having therapy would become depressed and take "just one little drink" in order to rid herself of the depression; after therapy she still became depressed but was able to choose not to take a drink of alcohol, although it was as available to her as before. She said, moreover, that she was now able to take one or two drinks and then quit, whereas formerly one or two drinks seemed to usher in a debauch which might last for days. It was also interesting to observe that she seemed to have re-defined the word "drink"; previous to therapy a "drink" was inevitably

alcoholic, while after therapy her thirst could be quenched by a non-intoxicating beverage.

6. We observe that our patients appear to be able to express their emotions more freely. There is definitely a lessening of inhibitory conduct with every therapy session, and our patients report that this also obtains in other interpersonal relationships. Nor does there seem to be any atrophy of the emotions; instead the reactions which seem to require an emotional potentiation are expressed with an appropriate emotion of appropriate intensity. An epileptic who appeared to have bottled-up rage reactions which were transformed into *grand mal* seizures was now able to express his anger verbally and actionally, when the situation warranted; as a concomitant the frequency of his attacks diminished from *grand mal* once a week to *petit mal* once in three months.

7. Our patients report that they have fewer guilt feelings, and our observation of their behavior seems to substantiate this. Previous conduct which was unwise or inexpedient is now evaluated factually and objectively; a past "misdeed" is regarded as a lesson, rather than as a cause for shame.

8. Our patients appear to learn to differentiate between an ideal and an actuality. There was a patient who had noticeably mixed feelings toward his father: on a verbal level he "hated" his father, yet it was observable that he frequently manifested behavior patterns which were typical of his paternal parent. After therapy he developed an attitude of understanding, and seemed to regard his father as a human being, no better and no worse than any of the rest of us, instead of reacting towards him as if he were a fiend in human form.

Another patient, who had previously been chronically unhappy, seemed to arrive at the realization that his wife was not the paragon of virtue he once mistook her for; by becoming aware of all the aspects of her conduct he could differentiate between the ideal wife who existed only in his imagination and the actual person to whom he was married. Instead of maintaining a compulsive dependency on her, he was able to divorce her with considerable equanimity.

9. We have observed a decrease in frequency and severity of numerous psychosomatic illnesses. Our group, since its inception, has treated patients with various allergies, migraine, epilepsy, chronic rhinitis and epistaxis, hypertension, *impotentia eregendi*, chronic vaginitis with leukorrhea, chronic fibrositis, asthenopia, chronic non-specific conjunctivitis, chronic prostatitis and exophthalmic goiter. In each case there has been an amelioration of symptoms.

One patient, with a history of asthma due to sensitivity to foods, was relieved of his symptoms after approximately six hours of therapy; there has been no recurrence within a period of seven months, in spite of the fact that he is now eating a completely unrestricted diet.

We have also had under treatment for a short period of time a man with an annular carcinoma of the rectum. It was interesting to observe that his personality pattern suggested the possibility of his neoplasm being on a psychosomatic basis. He reported that there was a slight change in his bowel function and in the distribution of his discomfort during the therapy. The therapeutic benefits obtained in the eight hours of therapy which he had were admittedly slight; prior to therapy he had been advised to have a colostomy, which he had refused on the grounds that he "would rather die than be cut up." After his four sessions he was able to make the decision to undergo surgery.

The results with this patient suggest that it might be of value to pursue further the possibility of there being a psychosomatic element in new-growths. Further investigation awaits the obtaining of patients who are willing to take the undeniable risks of such a therapeutic approach.

10. We have also observed a rather uniform pattern of characterologic changes, a general modification of behavior-pattern: our patients seem to be more adaptable, more tolerant, and more considerate. On the other hand, behavior previously characterized by a syndrome which included over-compliance and propitiation has been replaced by independence and decisiveness. There is a greater willingness to admit one's own shortcomings, yet without any exaggeration of self-abasement. There is a tendency towards more considered judgment before reacting, as if the patient respected the old adage, "Think before you speak." There is a diminution of egocentricity and narcissistic self-concern and an increase in interest in exterior events.

It should be emphasized that these observations and results are those which have been obtained in our group and have been under my personal observation, and that they are not to be confused with the results reported by any other group, including the Hubbard Dianetic Research Foundation. The group feels that it would be inaccurate to compare our methods and results with those of other workers; there have been so many modifications in hypothesis and technique that we are not, strictly speaking, practicing classical dianetic therapy. Our approach is definitely more eclectic.

Nor do I feel that dianetics is the *only* method of treating illness. It would be foolhardy to discard old knowledge just because one has new information; it is equally reprehensible, from the scientific viewpoint, to cling to older methodologies when newer ones give promise of greater efficacy. The approach outlined in this book will someday, I hope, be incorporated into the general body of knowledge of human beings, in the same manner in which psychoanalysis was adopted and in which general semantics, cybernetics, etc. are now being assimilated.

The possibility that dianetics is capable of assimilation into medicine is emphasized in a letter recently received from a Doctor of Medicine who is doing research in biophysics at Johns Hopkins University. I quote excerpts: "One of the very intriguing things to me about dianetics is the fact that you can tie certain of its basic concepts down to definite parts of the brain. . . . One can tie the analyzer and the reactive mind down to definite brain structures with known or probable connections and properties that are just what one would expect from dianetic theory. But where, oh where can one find the Superego, the Ego, or the Id? . . . It should be noted that sensory impulses *do* reach the cerebral cortex when an animal is under anesthesia; this fact should, I think, be emphasized as showing that 'recording while unconscious' is not only possible but probable. . . . When two independent approaches [dianetics and neurophysiology] to the same underlying reality using different techniques yield parallel results, one is justified in concluding that both approaches are probably sound and that the results are probably correct."

OTHER INVESTIGATIONS

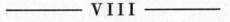 VIII

So far I have told of the observations in dianetics which have been proved to be useful, and I have told of the technique which has been developed as a result of these observations. This report would be incomplete if I did not tell of the other observations which were not followed up or which did not seem to lead to therapeutic usefulness.

The observation which would appear to have the greatest potential value revolves around the device known as "the file-clerk." Hubbard has chosen to anthropomorphize certain functions of the mind; the function of seeking out one specific datum from all the data which had been recorded, or finding one specific experience among those of a lifetime, was seen to be similar to the activities of a file-clerk, and was therefore so designated. In the Hubbardian technique, the auditor addresses the file-clerk when he wants information and manipulates this function as if it were a discrete entity.

Another similar device, used in conjunction with the anthropomorphic file-clerk was the "somatic strip." This developed from Hubbard's observation that the portion of the mind which seemed to store the recording of pain could be manipulated separately. If the time-track were made up of strips on which the perception-recordings were registered, that strip which dealt with pain and discomfort ("somatics") could be called the "somatic strip."

It was common practice in the Foundation to direct the patient in therapy by saying, "The file-clerk will hand up the incident we need next and the somatic strip will go to the earliest moment of discomfort." A patient who had been well-indoctrinated in Hubbardian terminology (or jargon, if you prefer) would usually respond by developing a sensation of discomfort in some portion of his anatomy.

I used this device but little, feeling that it was unnecessary and perhaps dangerous. It was my belief that any psychotherapy should act to integrate the various functions of the mind, and that splitting off one function in order to control other functions could be considered tantamount to training the patient in schizophrenia. It seemed, moreover, as I mentioned previously, that the device of designating a function by a personification could lead to semantic confusion, making the indoctrination of a patient needlessly complicated. It is a commentary on the marvelous functioning of the human mind that such a device works at all.

There was one extremely interesting offshoot from this idea of a separate entity within the mind, one which might well be worth further serious investigation. It was found that at the end of a session, if the following suggestion were made: "Until the next session the file-clerk will continue to hand up somatics and the somatic strip will sweep over them until the somatic is erased," the majority of patients would respond in a typical manner. They would feel a pain first in one part of the body, then another, then another and so on until it seemed as if they were re-experiencing all the pains they had ever had. Then they would re-experience these pains again, not necessarily in the same order. The process would continue, and some of the pains would diminish and disappear.

One instance which was reported to me was the case of a girl who had had idiopathic epilepsy; previous electroencephalograms had shown the characteristic tracings. She was given another EEG while in the process of "running somatics" as described in the previous paragraph; she stated that she was having mild headaches of a few seconds duration several times a minute. It was reported that the tracings obtained during these headaches were similar to those obtained during a full-blown epileptiform seizure, although the patient was apparently perfectly conscious and was amused by the consternation of the technician who was taking the EEG.

In spite of the bizarre terminology used in giving the suggestion to the patient, it seems likely that we have evidence here of a function of the mind which might profitably be investigated. I hesitate to predict that any therapeutic benefits could be obtained from utilization of this process; yet that possibility exists whenever we are able to manipulate a function. Perhaps it is possible to train a portion of the mind to act as a therapist for the remainder of the mind; it might even be that that is what we are doing in therapy. It is my hope that someone will someday try to find out where this observation leads.

For about a month I carried on a short and cursory investigation of the effects of oxygen and carbon dioxide as an adjunct to dianetic therapy. I had had the opportunity of watching Dr. Paul Wilcox of the Michigan State Hospital at Traverse City give a demonstration of his "psycho-penetration" technique. His method is to give the patient five or ten breaths of a mixture of 20% CO_2 and 80% O_2—a modification of Meduna's original technique. Wilcox's hypothesis is that *no* sensory stimulation can result from this amount of this mixture; the patients, however, report a peculiar smell or a taste or a sense of dizziness. He feels that these sensations are perception-memories of events which occurred in the patient's past, and he investigates these associations in the conventional psychoanalytic manner.

At the close of the session he re-administers the gas mixture and notes what the patient reports. If the gas no longer provokes a perception-response, it is concluded that this association is no longer of importance to the patient—"insight" has been obtained.

I made about 25 or 30 observations of this method, giving the patient five or ten breaths, noting the report of altered sensation, then asking for a phrase which might be associated with the strongest sensation. Wilcox's observations were confirmed by my experience.

Most of the patients observed had previously been well-indoctrinated in the tenets of Hubbardian dianetics, and I therefore hesitate to place value on the associations brought up by this technique as distinguished from reactions obtained in ordinary dianetic therapy. Most of them said, however, that the sense of discomfort was reached more quickly and with a greater sense of reality when the gas was used.

The testing for reduction of discomfort by administering the gas a second time was useful in one case; a patient had had considerable previous therapy without the usual amount of improvement in her general condition. I had suspected for some time that the incidents she reviewed were more fictional than factual; she claimed that in her "prenatal" incidents she could see what was going on outside her mother's body,

a phenomenon frequently observed in patients who are removed from reality.

With the first administration of the gas she reported a
marked dyspnea, an inner trembling and an undulatory
feeling. She reviewed an incident in her usual manner, showing none of the signs of reduction such as yawning, stretching
and diminution of bodily tension. With the second administration of the gas, she reported that her sensations of dyspnea, etc., were stronger. It was pointed out to her that her
response, theoretically, indicated that the incident she had
reviewed was not factually valid; what did she think about
that? She became quite nervous and emotionally upset,
whereupon she was put back into the therapy situation by her
usual therapist. He reported at the close of this session that,
for the first time since he had been working with her, she
apparently had reached a valid incident. With the third
administration of gas the sensations had disappeared.

Another patient who had not had any previous dianetic
therapy was observed. He was given five breaths of O_2-CO_2,
after which he reported a sense of breathlessness and a tendency to breathe deeply, a pungent odor and a slight dizziness.
I asked him to notice the dizziness and to give me the first
phrase he thought of, to which he replied, "I really can't think
of anything." A few moments silence, then he said, "My head
feels like it's detached from my body; I feel like I'm hanging
from my feet. My God, can this be my birth?"

I asked, "What do you suppose is being said here?" He
reported that the words, "Now it's coming. Here it is. Here
you are," occurred to him, and that he also felt chilly all over
and had a headache. I had him repeat these phrases until the
headache diminished (I have made some changes in my
methods since then) and then re-administered the gas. He then
reported the same pungent odor, which he now identified as

chloroform, and a similar sense of breathlessness; the dizziness did not recur.

The patient's interpretation of this was that he had re-experienced some of the sensations and had recalled some of the words which had been spoken at the time of his birth.

My general impression of this CO_2 technique is that it seems useful, especially in those cases where the patient finds it difficult to re-experience pain. I tend to disagree with Meduna's contention that the gas mixture itself gives therapeutic benefits; moreover, I am not convinced that it is the carbon dioxide alone which causes the observed results—the tripling or quadrupling of the percentage of oxygen in the pulmonary atmosphere might also have some effects, a possibility which Meduna has apparently overlooked.

I did not pursue this course of investigation longer but deferred further investigation until I had re-examined some of the basic tenets of dianetics. I felt that simply using this medication as an adjunct to Hubbardian dianetics was not giving me the information for which I was searching. There were still too many gaps in the hypothesis, too many unexplained observations. Some of the explanations for relative failures in therapy were more ingenious than explanatory. The uncritical use of such "gimmicks" as the file-clerk seemed to be stultifying to further advancement of knowledge.

The attitude within the Foundation by this time (September, 1950) also seemed to preclude the possibility of further serious research. It was my hope, when the Foundation was set up, that we were creating an organization which would attract a group of serious, interested, scientifically-trained persons to work together in an effort to increase our knowledge of the functioning of the mind. I felt that the fresh viewpoint of the dianetic hypothesis would be useful in discovering new avenues of research.

I found, moreover, that I had made the error of generalizing from insufficient data when I subscribed to Hubbard's belief that "any two reasonably intelligent people" can practice dianetics on each other. Subsequent observation of the students at the Foundation led me to conclude that something more than enthusiasm for a new idea was needed to make a good therapist.

The investigations sponsored by the Foundation—or, as they called it, the "research program"—were also a source of dissatisfaction to me. For example, considerable time and effort were spent in investigating the possible therapeutic benefits of "recalling" the circumstances of deaths in previous incarnations; the suggestion that such a "recollection" might be an asynchronic synthesis was scoffed at, and these fantasies were deemed to be as real as a memory of the day before yesterday. I had no objection to seeing patients consider a "past death" as an exercise in fantasy synthesis (a technique which Jung has long claimed to have therapeutic benefit) or as an approach to a real situation via the imagination route— but to give to these highly improbable events the evaluation of complete reality was to me an indication of a lack of scientific scepticism.

Investigation of the "past death"—or the "last death" in less imaginative patients—had only a brief popularity. It was replaced by the "sperm-ovum" sequence, which was defined as the "recollections" of occurrences at the moment of a person's conception. This was again evaluated as being of sufficient reality as to make it a part of the Foundation's standard auditing procedure.

A "sperm dream," as I prefer to call this phenomenon, is occasionally seen in the course of therapy. A typical example will be described in detail in the next chapter. Such dreams are highly interesting, both to the patient and the therapist, but our present knowledge of structure makes their actual reality highly improbable.

And then there was the "Guk" program: "Guk" was the name given to a haphazard mixture of vitamins and glutamic acid, which was taken in huge doses in the belief that it made the patient "run better." There were no adequate controls set up for this experiment, and it was a dismal, expensive failure. My objections to such uncritical "research," as well as my efforts to put dianetic research on a more sound and scientific basis were unavailing, and I was led to infer that I was acting as a deterrent to the progress of the Foundation.

The manner in which the Foundation was evolving became increasingly divergent from my views as to what constituted a serious scientific organization. When I began to investigate dianetics, my opinion was as follows: here we have a new hypothesis of function of the human mind, and a system of therapy based on that hypothesis. By means of it, we could explain many previously inexplicable phenomena, and further generalizations could be made which could embrace other previously unrelated zones of human activity. Dianetics, in short, appealed to me as a useful and usable working hypothesis, one which could be tentatively accepted as a basis for further investigation.

The Foundation, in contrast, seemed to regard the dianetic hypothesis as the *ne plus ultra* of thinking about thought, and it soon became apparent that Foundation dianetics was becoming crystallized, ritualistic and sterile. The policies of this organization also included a none-too-subtle antagonism towards the medical profession in general and the psychiatric field in particular. I felt, and I still believe, that any benefits to the human race which dianetics has to offer will be secured by absorption of this newer viewpoint into the body of existing medical knowledge. Furthermore, any attempts to force the medical profession to accept it solely on the basis of the affirmation, "It works!" and deriding those who request more conclusive proof, is more than likely to jeopardize whatever possible benefits there might be.

I made numerous attempts at different times to put Foundation policies on a more reasoned and conservative basis, but my efforts were rebuffed. In the hope that I might be able to rescue the therapeutically useful portions of dianetics from the welter of the Foundation's chauvinism, I resigned in order to carry out further research under more propitious circumstances.

THE PRESENT PHASE

―――――― IX ――――――

IN DECEMBER OF 1950, I opened an office for the practice of psychosomatic medicine in New York City. I chose to refer to my practice in this way because I did not feel that I was going to practice dianetics exclusively—certainly not in the Foundation sense of the word. Working with me were two associates, Nancy Roodenburg, a former lay analyst, and Myron Beigler, one of the first graduates of the Foundation training school.

Our group was unanimous in its dissatisfaction with Hubbardian dianetics, but agreed in the belief that a useful psychotherapeutic method could be developed from it. It was our intent to re-investigate the methods and techniques of other schools of psychology, using the dianetic hypothesis as a measuring stick, with the idea that some sound contributions could ultimately be made. The technique which has been described in detail elsewhere in this book is essentially the work of our group.

In addition to my practice, I conducted a seminar for a

group of psychoanalysts, in which the medical profession and the laity were both represented. The free interchange of experience and opinion which ensued was tremendously stimulating to me, and I was able to detect a similar stimulation among the other members of the seminar. The opinion was expressed that this new technique would compensate for some of the admitted deficits of psychoanalysis, and was well worthy of further investigation and use.

Among the patients treated by our group were cases of illness which could be classified as psychosomatic, and others which could be called neuroses. These conventional categories, I find, have lost their usefulness; with the basic assumption that the mind is the function of the entire body, any illness which occurs in the absence of recent chemical, mechanical, thermal, electrical or bacterial injury is considered as the result of mental dysfunction.

The results were encouraging. A patient who had had epilepsy for years reported that his attacks, which occurred previously on the average of once a week, after therapy, occurred less than once a month. At last observation, he had gone for six weeks without a seizure.

A patient with chronic nasal hemorrhage reported that her nose-bleeds had ceased. A man with chronic allergic rhinitis noticed a disappearance of his nasal symptoms. A patient who had had nocturnal enuresis for years reported that the incidence of bed-wetting had decreased. These results were obtained in twenty hours of therapy or less. Many other cases are, of course, in progress with noticeable benefit; however, since the period of observation has been short, I do not feel that unqualified claims could as yet be considered scientifically valid.

An extremely interesting case was reported to me by a man associated with our group. His father had been injured accidentally, having been struck on the head by a piece of stone falling from a cornice. Although none of the medical details are available to me, I inferred that the patient had sustained, at the very least, a severe cerebral concussion. My friend saw his father about 14 hours after the accident, at which time he was still unconscious and unmoving.

Using the method of permissive positive suggestion, the patient was told, quietly and repetitively, "You can wake up if you want to. You can open your eyes. You can speak. You can move. You can remember what happened." Within less than a half-hour, the patient had regained consciousness, was moving and speaking with apparently little difficulty. His recovery thereafter was rapid, and within four days, he had returned to work with no evidence of sequelae or complaints.

Such a case is mentioned partially as an indication of the efficacy of our methods, which we find encouraging. Even more important is the fact that these results offer suggestive evidence of the existence of a hitherto unexploited function of the mind, a function which can be manipulated to produce effects. It is much too early to determine the scope of disease processes which can be treated, or to ascertain how permanent the results will be. The effects subsequent, if not consequent, are sufficiently striking to encourage me to pursue this course of investigation further, and to make it justifiable to report these observations to those who deal with mental as well as somatic functioning.

There is one case in particular which I should like to report in greater detail, as an exposition of methodology, an example of the sort of information which a patient might bring up, and as an illustration of the results obtained.

S. C., a white female, age 48, born in U.S.A., of native American parents, had been married and divorced twice, the precipitating causes of both divorces being marital infidelity of her husbands. There were three siblings, an older brother who died at patient's age 32, and a younger brother and sister.

Her chief complaint was high blood-pressure, first discovered ten years previously when she noticed an impairment of function of the left side of her body and persistent lachrymation of the left eye.

Report of findings and diagnosis by her family physician as of 24 July 1950, four months before inception of treatment:

"1. Hypertension, the average of multiple observations before treatment being 230/134.
2. Cardiac enlargement.
3. Hemiplegia 1938 and again in 1948.
4. Absence of right kidney, probably congenital.
5. Impaired renal function.
6. Diabetic glucose tolerance curve with normal fasting blood sugar.
7. Obesity.
    The patient was treated by Veratrum Viride, and by the Kempner Rice Diet. On this treatment during her hospital stay, the blood-pressure subsided to 161/91 (an average of many days observation) and on subsequent ambulation, the average reading was 174/112. She has undertaken weight reduction along with the diet, and has lost a total of 42 pounds." (Weight was not given.)

On her first visit to me, on December 5, 1950, her weight was 247 pounds, and her blood-pressure was 240/160. Her flow of conversation was frequently circumstantial and disconnected. She manifested anxiety about whether or not I would "take her case"; the assurance that I would elicited verbalizations of relief but an observable increase in anxiety as manifested by her conversational rate.

A summary of each of her therapy sessions follows:

5 December. Asked patient what she thought about her health; she answered: "Nothing to it. I never gave it any room in my mind; I believed in carrying on." Identified these phrases as typical of her maternal grandmother. Recalled a scene at age 9, when grandmother tapped her on the right side of her head with a thimble, saying, "It's all right." Patient was able to re-experience this trivial discomfort, which disappeared on several recountings.

On developing further recollections of this event, patient stated that grandmother was encouraging her because her mother had expressed her dislike of patient's singing. Patient said that she was not her mother's favorite. She stated that she was able to recall her grandmother's voice tones vividly, but not her mother's.

THERAPIST: Can you recall a time when you felt that you triumphed over your mother?

PATIENT: I remember a time when I walked home from school with a girl whom mother disliked. She met me at the door and struck me. "You're with that girl again. I told you not to walk with her." I kicked my mother. She said, "You hurt my legs—my poor veins! I'll get you for this!"

Patient recalled details of this scene fully, including the pain of being struck. It was noticeable, however, that there was no manifestation of anger toward the mother; the patient's affect level did not change.

Patient was asked about literal meanings of phrases and how they might affect her, if she were to apply them to herself. She saw a parallelism between mother's "hurt legs" and her own difficulties in walking; between mother's "poor veins" and her own cerebral vascular accident.

THERAPIST: You can remember, if you want to. You know the difference between yourself and your mother, don't you? You don't have to have poor veins or hurt legs just because your mother did.

7 December. Patient reported feeling stronger physically; she noted some confusion of thinking, however, since previous session. BP 240/160.

PATIENT: If I could only be more trustworthy; I'm not so sure that I can be truthful. Hold me tight to the truth— I'm weak.

Any one of these self-judgments, which according to our premise probably stem from some aberrative event, could have been investigated. Because of the nature of her illness and her complaints, the following question was asked.

THERAPIST: Who was weak?

PATIENT: My first husband.

Several specific examples of his "weakness" were reviewed. It was noted that the patient made no mention of how his conduct affected her.

THERAPIST: How do you feel about this?

PATIENT: I felt hurt—like crying inwardly; but I didn't let on.

THERAPIST: Try to recall an earlier incident of weakness, where you were crying inwardly but not letting on.

PATIENT: I remember when Father broke Mother's heart—in a way.

THERAPIST: What did your father do?

PATIENT: He went with a lewd woman.

THERAPIST: How do you feel about this?

PATIENT: I don't feel a darn thing. I don't care.

THERAPIST: If you could feel something, what would you feel?

After a few moments patient reported a pleasurable sensation in her genitalia and a feeling of generalized tension.

THERAPIST: What words go with this sensation?

PATIENT: "It's heavy on my stomach. (Laughter.) I liked it. Let's leave it."

She also reported a generalized tingling sensation after several repetitions of these words. At this point the session was interrupted when the patient reported a strong pressure sensation in her right flank, the site of the non-functioning kidney; it became necessary to her to empty her bladder. She reported that an unusually large amount of urine was passed.

THERAPIST: Try to return to the incident you were recalling before the interruption. What do you suppose is going on?

PATIENT: Father and mother having intercourse.

THERAPIST: What might they be saying?

PATIENT: "Silly—you couldn't have mistaken it. It feels good. That was a dandy. That finishes me."

The scene was reviewed until the generalized tension had disappeared. Patient interpreted "That finishes me" as a possible death-threat: something which finishes me equals death; this phrase was said during coitus; ergo, coitus equals death.

Blood pressure at end of session 240/130.

9 December. Patient reported that she felt stronger and could walk better; less confusion in her thinking. Wt. 247 lbs. BP 204/140.

THERAPIST: What do you remember about your mother's death?

Patient recalled this event in considerable detail, but with no manifestation of affect. She mentioned also that her brother and sister were present at her mother's death.

THERAPIST: Have you any idea as to why you didn't cry?

PATIENT: I try to suppress my emotions.

THERAPIST: How do you feel about your brother and sister?

PATIENT: My sister bothers me; we don't think alike. I'm ashamed of her. They don't understand; they have so much to learn.

The remainder of the session was spent in trying to establish patient's dramatization of anger, and it was found that she apparently had no adequate way of expressing this emotion.

THERAPIST: What do you do when you're provoked?

PATIENT: I just toss my head—smile and walk away.

Further inquiry revealed that the gesture of tossing the head was typical of her mother. Continued attempts were made to have her review various times when she was angry and to have her act out this emotion; patient was cooperative and compliant but gave no sign of affect.

The impression of this patient at this time was that she was verbally compliant, actionally resistant. The emotion of anger was given no outlet; the tentative conclusion, therefore, was that one factor in her hypertension was unexpressed rage. There was, moreover, a confusion between rage and pleasure as manifested by smiling. Nor did she have any outlet for the emotion of grief. She was able to express pleasure, judged by her behavior in recalling the "coitus event" of the previous session.

14 December.

THERAPIST: How do you feel?

PATIENT: I felt depressed and down in the dumps since the last session. Today I feel childish and full of mischief. Slap me down—don't let me get away with anything—make me obey you.

An attempt was made to develop the concept contained in these remarks, without success. It was then suggested that the patient try to recall the incident of her father's death. She reported a premonition of his death: at a social gathering she saw her father's face superimposed on the face of one of the guests; she also became aware of acting as her father did. Her father's death had occurred while she was abroad, and she was not notified until her return, when her husband informed her.

THERAPIST: What was your response to this news?

PATIENT: I sat there holding it in—I wouldn't face it. I said, "Thank you, but I knew." I was afraid to say more.

Patient showed no evidence of emotion.

THERAPIST: Do you feel like crying?

PATIENT: No, I guess he was better off dead.

THERAPIST: What do you think about a person who cries?

PATIENT: He's a sissy.

The phrase "better off dead" was investigated; this brought up a threat of suicide at age 24, which was reviewed in detail.

Patient was then asked to try to recall an earlier event of similar pattern. She soon reported a sensation of generalized trembling.

PATIENT: "I hate it, and I'm not going to have it. Why

do I have to go through with it? Why must it be? I wish there was something I could do. I wonder. . . . I'm not going to have it and that's all there is to it."

Patient identified these words as her mother's, with the incident being from her prenatal period when her mother was depressed and suicidal because of her pregnancy. The mood was one of both anger and grief. The incident was reviewed until the sensation of trembling had disappeared. Patient was asked how she would obey these various phrases, assuming that they were commands.

THERAPIST: Who is "it"? Could "it" be you? Does "I hate it" mean that you have to hate yourself? You can obey these commands or not, as you prefer. You can "have it" or not, as you wish.

Patient made the appropriate responses to these permissive suggestions and finished the session in a noticeably cheerful and resolute mood.

16 December.   Patient reported that she had been busy since last session; there was an increasing clarity of thinking, but she said, "I still can't keep my mind on things." She reported that she could walk better and was able to stand straighter, also that she had had a dream of coitus, culminating in orgasm.

This session began with a discussion of punishment, in an attempt to follow up the "slap me down" comment of the previous session.

THERAPIST: What are the advantages of being punished?

PATIENT: It brings relief; the situation is eliminated.

It was noted that the patient seemed unable to approach this subject of punishment, so the "drama" gambit was tried. After numerous false starts and comments leading away from this topic, the patient constructed a drama of a man punishing a woman, with the following dialogue:

MAN: You low-down chippy. You cheated on me.

WOMAN: So what? I liked it; it's better than you ever gave me. I'll do it again if I get the chance.

Patient comments that after the quarrel they have coitus. She was asked to elaborate this dialogue further, which elicited:

MAN: (Pounds woman on abdomen.) You whore. You're cheap. You've been running around. Where have you been?

WOMAN: You god-damned son of a bitch. You hit me. You let me alone. Don't you know I'm pregnant?

MAN: What does that matter? You're no good. I'll kill the bastard if I can get ahold of him.

WOMAN: You'll never know. He was better than you.

Patient said at this point, "She hits me." She reviewed this dialogue several times, becoming quite animated. When asked for further dialogue, she added:

WOMAN: Damn you—you'll make me lose the baby.

MAN: I want to; you'll never carry a son of mine. I'll kill you.

WOMAN: Darling, you don't mean that. Let's be together. Oh, how you can kiss. Let's try again. You know you love me.

As pointed out in previous chapters, this device is used in order to pick up phrases associated with a specific behavior pattern, phrases with which an incident may be entered. There is no suspicion that such a scene was ever actually played, either by the patient or by her parents. We do consider, however, that motivations and mood-responses characteristic of the patient can be exposed, and that the exaggerated vulgarity of the language acts to release affect. It is interesting to note that the patient chose to have her characters end their angry quarrel with coitus; compare this with her pattern of smiling during anger.

Patient was asked to repeat the phrase, "You god-damned whore." There was no response to this repetition; patient commented, "I'm sorry, but there's no response. The poor girl— she couldn't help it."

Next phrase to be repeated was, "You know you love me." I chose this phrase for the reason that, if there had been a quarrel in her past experience similar to the quarrel in her drama, this phrase would probably appear near the end of the incident. In working into a scene of emotional intensity, it is often easier to pick the less painful portion and work backwards towards the moment of maximum pain.

After several repetitions, patient added the phrases, "Love me just like the devil. I'm weak—forgive me. Don't ever leave me." With further repetition, the patient became extremely somnolent. It was necessary for me to raise my voice before she would respond to my request to repeat. It was also observed that at first these words were attributed to her mother; as the patient's somnolence decreased, she attributed the words to her father. She finally modified them to, "You know you love me darling. You couldn't get along without me and I couldn't get along without you."

With this, patient reported a strong feeling of sexual stimulation, which did *not* diminish in intensity with repetition. She also said she had a feeling of a swaying motion, being in a dark moist place and an impression of laughter. Patient assumed the foetal position.

Suddenly, without suggestion from me, she reported the following, which was taken down *verbatim:* "I feel like I'm traveling upwards; as if I was a tadpole in a vagina. I have a feeling in my vagina. Then there's the feeling of hitting something, as if it arrives. These feelings are within. Then it's sealed—it feels like a trowel is closing something over. There is a speck of light—a tiny pinpoint of light. It goes—it's dark. There is a feeling here (points to upper abdomen) of quickness—of aliveness. I have a sensation of awareness, of invigoration in my abdomen."

Patient was asked to go through this event again.

"It's dark, except for a tiny little ray. There's a sudden flick of nausea—as though it was the beginning of sensation. It's getting more intensive. I'm feeling a quickening, tingling sensation—it's pleasant—in my left side and hands—going through my body—up to my head. It's going all through. There's something in the darkness—just like my conception years ago of inertia (circular motion with right hand). It's going around—upward. It can't grow that quickly—darn it. I feel—that I'm taking a position—as if I were a mass of something. Mass—mass—it's moving—larger. It's swinging, curving. (Any discomfort?) There's no discomfort—it doesn't seem to be attached—but it seems to be higher, rather than lower—slightly to the left of center. Like a half-circle. There's a slight rocking motion. It feels as if it's enclosed—covered—in something else."

After several recountings of this, with no essential variation, she suddenly reported, "It's gone." Session was thereupon ended. Patient reported that she was dizzy; she appeared confused and not well oriented.

This session has been reported in great detail as an example of the bizarre and inexplicable events which are occasionally observed, and which are referred to as the "sperm dream." This dreamlike fantasy or allegory, call it what you wish, is quite characteristic, and occurs in nearly every patient some time in the course of therapy, regardless of intellectual level or degree of disturbance. I shall make no attempt to evaluate or interpret it. It might be said, however—and I say this with due caution—that if a person were to remember what transpired at the time of his own conception, his recollections might well be similar to this.

On the other hand, there are numerous other possible explanations, of which I am well aware. Most people have a general idea of the morphology of the spermatozoon and know something about the physiology of conception. At various times in their lives they have experienced the feeling of traveling upwards, the feelings of moisture, darkness, sexual excitement, etc. In other words, there is a sufficient amount of data from other experiences to construct the "imaginative" synthesis as reported here.

I have not observed any effect on the patient's therapy, either beneficial or deleterious, from encountering such a scene. It is my practice, however, to have the patient repeat it until any sensation of discomfort which might be associated with it has disappeared.

19 December.   BP 230/130. During this session, the patient appeared unable to remain in any specific incident. She recalled and reviewed the scene in which she separated from her second husband.

THERAPIST: What does he say?

PATIENT: "I don't know what I'll do without you. Please don't leave me. I'm no damn good."

THERAPIST: What is your reaction to this?

PATIENT: I just can't go on any longer. I can't carry such a burden. I'm angry and reckless. I don't care—but I'm not quite truthful. I'm tired of protecting everyone; I've got to get away.

Towards the end of the session, the patient expressed the thought that her mother might have tried to get rid of her pre-natally. She had read Hubbard's book, in which he states that attempted abortions are frequently "contacted," and that they are the source of many aberrations. She wondered if such a thing might not have occurred in her prenatal existence; my response was that, if there were such an event, she could re-member it. The pattern of the patient's personality was be-coming more clear, to her as well as to me. It was as if she needed to be punished, that it was incumbent upon her to have a husband who would be "weak" and adulterous. Her optimum survival pattern was repression of expression of all emotions except sweet, smiling compliance. There was a smoldering rage behind her facade of propitiation, and I felt that she was becoming aware of this.

21 December.   As the patient took her position on the couch at the start of the session, she said, "Now if I'm wrong, slap me down."

She was asked to return to a time when she was slapped down; it was observed that she immediately put her hand to the left side of her face. There were no associations im-mediately forthcoming, so another gambit was used with the following ensuing:

THERAPIST: What do you think about being slapped down?

PATIENT: I like being slapped down if I need it.

THERAPIST: Under what circumstances might a person need to be slapped down?

PATIENT: He might need it when he overstepped the traces —in order to be taught—if he disobeyed a command—if he didn't follow a set pattern—if he became angry.

Any one of these associations could have been followed up

with probable benefit; I chose to investigate the anger, because of my impression that her unexpressed anger was a factor in her hypertension.

THERAPIST: Suppose you were going to slap somebody down because he became angry; what would you say to him?

PATIENT: I don't like to do this—I regret it, but that's the way it is—I think I'd just smile and let it go.

THERAPIST: What else might you say?

PATIENT: Don't—it isn't worth it. Why do you do such a thing? It's beneath you. You shouldn't do it. But I don't quarrel—I restrain myself and retain things within.

(Apropos of this last remark, in a previous discussion with her she had mentioned that her obesity was due, she felt, to a retention of fluids, and that she consistently noted that her urinary output was scanty except immediately after each session.)

THERAPIST: Of what does this remind you?

PATIENT: Of a quarrel with my brother. I gave up everything for him. If I can only pull it—it's a little thing.

Note the apparent irrelevance of the last sentence. It could be construed as meaning, "If I could only pull out the memories of this quarrel—it's an event of minor importance." According to the theory, however, these are words derived from an earlier situation, similarized to the event under discussion by virtue of parallel affect-pattern or pain-pattern.

She was asked to recall the quarrel with her brother, which she did in detail.

THERAPIST: What does he say?

PATIENT: "If you're going to boss me, we're not going to get along." I just said, "I'm sorry—I quit."

THERAPIST: How do you feel about this?

PATIENT: I feel like sinking through the floor. I couldn't believe what he was saying. I feel inwardly twisted and churned up. I haven't time to give to it to work it out.

She was asked to return to the first time she felt this way, giving me whatever words occurred to her.

PATIENT: It's mother; she says, "I can't get it. I must give up. It hurts. It's no use—I can't do it—I'd better quit. I can't stand it. It's wrong. What's the use?"

Associated sensations were darkness, a lifting motion, a feeling of moisture over the entire body and generalized pressure. She identified this scene as an attempt at self-induced abortion by her mother. She was asked to go over these words repeatedly, and add any other associations which might occur. She finally added the sounds of sobbing, and after a few repetitions of that sound she broke into uproarious laughter. When asked again for the words, she said that she could not remember what they were, nor could she recall the sensations previously reported.

There are several aspects to this session which require discussion. What about these attempted abortions which Hubbard discussed so freely? My experience in practicing medicine taught me that attempted abortions are frequent, perhaps more frequent among married than among unmarried women. I know also that women with an unwanted pregnancy will sometimes make half-hearted attempts to rid themselves of their uterine contents, then desist after a few unsuccessful attempts. Granted that the foetus can record and recall prenatal experiences, one would expect that an attempted abortion would contain data which would be evaluated as tremendously important to survival.

On the other hand, I am also aware of the tendency of patients to grasp at suggested positive explanations, to act in a manner which might be expressed as, "Well, Hubbard says that there are a lot of attempted abortions; maybe I'd better try to run one." This patient had read Hubbard's book, so the possibility that this event was in response to a suggestion, rather than spontaneous, must be considered.

What was done, of course, was to accept this "recollection" as being valid; the impossibility of securing information to corroborate it leaves no other alternative, and the benefits to the patient do not seem to hinge on the validity. It was, at least, valid to the patient, and it is with the patient's own internal reality that the therapist must deal if he is to present alternative possibilities.

The patient also manifested the phenomenon called "erasure," wherein the verbal content disappeared from recall, along with the associated sensations of discomfort. According to Hubbard, this disappearance is permanent. Experience with this patient and with others has shown that these experiences, complete with discomfort, may be touched upon several times in the course of therapy, although their content may temporarily be lost as above described.

23 December. Discussion of the patient's progress at the opening of the session brought up the following comments: "My weight remains constant. I seem to be retaining liquids. I have the urge to cooperate all I can, because of your standing. I've always tried to do my part. I've always bent over backwards trying to do everything to the letter. I've often wanted to pull up stakes, but I had to keep going, no matter what it cost. I tried to work the darn thing out."

She was asked to repeat the phrase, "I'm trying to work the darn thing out." After numerous repetitions, interrupted by the comments, "To me that means life," and "I still have farther to go before the turning," she suddenly asked, "What's going on?" She reported a sudden release of tension over her entire body, which she said felt like being rejuvenated.

THERAPIST: If these words hurt you, where would they hurt?

PATIENT: In my mind. I'm having a feeling of discomfort in the left side of my forehead.

THERAPIST: Do any other words occur to you?

PATIENT: "It seems hopeless; I can't get it."

She then recalled an event at the age of 7, a fall out of a tree.

THERAPIST: Where is the discomfort?

PATIENT: I hurt all over, especially my left side. I'm too proud to cry. I didn't dare tell mother—she'd scold. I feel alone. I'm ashamed and humiliated to have fallen, to be hurt. It hurts so much that I could cry—but I don't want the children to know.

This reminded her of her mother's "sick headaches," which were characterized by prostration, nausea and vomiting. On being asked to return to the first experience of "sick headache," she reported a feeling of constriction and the words, "I'm so sick. I'm too ill to bother." This was repeated until the sensation of constriction disappeared.

28 December. During the preliminary discussion, for no apparent appropriate reason, she inquired if she had made me angry or embarrassed. She either could not or would not give a reason for her asking this question; it was interpreted as a projection of her own feelings, although this explanation was not discussed with her.

Her first recollection in this session was of a time when she was 19; coming down in an elevator after a dance, she suddenly found it difficult to walk in a straight line; she would keep going towards the left, as if she had no control over herself. This was the same sort of feeling that she had later, after her first stroke in 1938. She also recalled that at the age of 13 her left side was smaller than her right; asked how she felt about this, she said, "I wondered about it, but I wouldn't give it much room."

THERAPIST: How does it feel to go down in an elevator?

PATIENT: It keys me up—lifts me. I feel wide open as though I lifted my forehead and expanded it.

Compare this statement with the observation that a baby's head is delivered by the neck being extended—a lifting of the forehead. This response, and others similar, could be interpreted as being in line with our observation that the feeling of falling or going down in an elevator seems to be associated with birth.

The remainder of this session seemed to be quite disorganized, as if she were simultaneously recalling events at numerous different times in her life. Verbal content included the phrases: "I can't get at the things I want; there's too much pressure. I don't dare love because I'll be stuck. There's no room to expand. My hands are tied . . . I wonder what I should do. I feel as if everything is at a standstill. There's nothing to it . . . It'll be all right. I'm caught. I don't know how to tell you. I'll have to chastise myself."

Towards the end of the session she brought up the phrases, "I'm just not going to have it. I'm going to tear it out, that's all there is to it." This was accompanied by a strong feeling of anger, which dissolved in laughter after numerous repetitions of the phrases.

From the reports of these sessions, the reader can infer what to expect. There is often a considerable amount of groping on the part of the patient, as if he is looking for a specific event which he is still unable to reach; in doing so, he becomes aware of the response-patterns of his lifetime. He will ultimately recall a specific experience in which he learned a lesson and developed an aberration, and the therapist assists him to as complete a recollection of it as possible.

It is noteworthy that it usually takes about an hour to get the patient to the point where he can grasp a definite experience; for this reason, it is our practice to schedule two-hour sessions. The first hour is spent in general exploration, the second in review of the material brought up in the first.

To sum up the particular case which we have discussed, the patient continued with the sessions twice a week until February 1. At that time, her blood-pressure was 200/116, a decrease of 44 mm. Hg. in the diastolic pressure. During this time she had been able to increase her activities with no ill effects; she was now able to climb on and off a bus with comparative ease. Her interests were no longer limited to herself. Her abilities to carry on a coherent conversation were improved. Her mood was now one of fun, rather than depression; as she expressed it, "I've got my sense of humor back." She was making plans for the future without worrying about her health.

On February 2, it was suggested that the patient be given a vacation from therapy, in order to permit the re-establishment of a balance, and to determine the relative permanency of the gains which were made. At an interview on May 9, 1951 she reported that her vision was better; she was able to read without glasses. She also mentioned that she was able to sing again, that the improvement in her ability to walk had been maintained, and that she was now able to "work things out for herself" and begin life over again.

It was also interesting to note that, on reading the report

of her case, she re-identified one of the phrases; during therapy she had placed this phrase in a "prenatal" setting but now identified it as being typical of her first husband. This suggests further the idea that "prenatal" memories might well be projections of recent experiences.

SUGGESTIONS FOR FURTHER
INVESTIGATION

———— X ————

I<small>T IS HOPED</small> that, after reading this book, some of my confrères will consider doing some further investigation of what appears to be a cogent hypothesis and a useful psychotherapeutic method. Some suggestions as to a possible starting-point might not be amiss.

A good demonstration of the efficacy of this technique is to have someone review a recent injury, as discussed on page 48. The technique of reviewing every possible sensation recording at the instant of reception of the injury should be obvious by now.

Another starting-point for investigation is to ask your patient or subject to return to a recent moment which was pleasurable. The method is described on page 86. Most people find it surprising to discover the amount of perceptual data which is recallable. Being accustomed to remembering abstractions of events, rather than the complete contents, tends to make one forget that he can recall the periphery as well as the focus of awareness.

We have seen some therapeutic effects ensue from the review of pleasure moments. At first glance, this should appear to be theoretically impossible; benefits are supposed to be obtained only from the reduction of pain. A case handled by one of my associates furnishes a good example of this. The patient complained of an extreme deficiency in sexual pleasure during marital relations; a previous marriage had ended in divorce because of her frigidity, and she had been contemplating a divorce from her second husband. The therapist asked her to recall a time when coitus was pleasurable, which she did with some difficulty. He simply took her through the event several times, asking her to become aware of all the sensations and thoughts which presented themselves. She was not asked to tell what went on, but merely to recall what had occurred, focussing her attention on each portion of the sensorium. He had her run through the entire event several times, then asked her to assume that it was one minute before her orgasm and to become aware of all the sensations at that instant; he then asked her to imagine that it was 45 seconds before orgasm and recall the cross-section of perceptions of that moment. Thirty seconds—fifteen seconds— the orgasm; at this point he could observe that she was breathing deeply and rapidly, that her face was flushed and that her body became slightly more tense, then relaxed. A half-dozen or so reviews were made in this manner: "It is a minute before you have your orgasm; now it's 45 seconds before; now it's 30 seconds—now it's 15 seconds—now it is the moment of the orgasm. Now let's go through it again: it's one minute. . . ." There was only one session with this patient, and this was the only incident touched upon. Moreover—and this is an interesting observation—there were *no* suggestions, either restrictive or permissive, given; the therapist at the conclusion of the session told the patient that it was an experiment and that he doubted that anything would happen.

A few weeks later, the young lady volunteered the information that her sex-life was "much better now." It was also observable that her personality had mellowed somewhat, and that her general appearance was more attractive. When this improvement in her appearance was commented on, she said, "I know the reason for that—I'm just taking better care of myself."

My explanation for the observable changes which had occurred are this: her educational and family background was of a religious nature; sex had been evaluated as "dirty" and "nasty," an unpleasant duty rather than an enjoyable experience. During coitus, she was aware of her *ideas* of sex, instead of directing her attention to the experience itself. The one session heightened her awareness of what goes on during coitus, and showed her that coitus did not have to be unenjoyable; she was thus enabled to differentiate between her own sensory experience and what she had been taught about coitus.

It seems obvious to me that a great deal of work can and should be done on the subject of "awareness" alone, and that the dianetic approach offers a useful methodology for further clinical investigation. What are the factors which go to make up "awareness"? What are the norms of the factors? What are the extremes? How can one objectively test "awareness"? Can the awareness potential be trained, and if so, how? What benefits can be obtained by increasing awareness? I am cognizant of the work which has been done along these lines, both in the field of General Semantics and in Gestalt Psychology, and am looking forward to further developments.

As previously mentioned, there is a considerable amount of testing which still needs to be done within the field of dianetics as it has been propounded. Only a relatively minor amount of objective data has been acquired as to the changes which ensue after dianetic therapy. I am frank to admit that my opinions as to the benefits obtained from therapy are the results of clinical impressions rather than objective evidence. Indeed, I am not entirely convinced that there are any tests extant which would be applicable to this sort of measurement.

As a start, however, it would be advisable to administer an entire battery of tests to a group of patients and a group of controls, retesting after two, ten, twenty and fifty hours of therapy, retesting again after a lapse of one month, six months, a year. The Rorschach, the Thematic Apperception and the Wechsler-Bellevue Tests seem to be the most appropriate tests to use at the outset. A sufficient number of controls should be kept to check on the "learning factor" in re-use of tests.

It is quite possible that such a study would reveal the need for developing new tests, and suggest certain attributes and functions for which there is no satisfactory testing procedure at present.

Another field of investigation which cries out for more research is the application of dianetic techniques to acute injuries and illnesses. In my family it is routine now to review every minor injury, any cuts, sprains, bruises or burns which occur accidentally to both children and adults. It is my impression that these injuries heal at an accelerated rate and with fewer complications after a dianetic review than without it. It would be most interesting to extend this methodology to the emergency room of the hospital, keeping a careful series of control cases, and obtain some definitive statistics.

Another research project which could be carried out in a

hospital would be to deliver a group of babies, using the precautions suggested by the findings of dianetic therapy. Minimum requirements for precautions would include absolute silence in the delivery room, illumination kept to the lowest feasible level, gentle handling of the baby with an avoidance of such procedures as holding him up by the ankles, and a caudal or sacral block anesthesia, rather than an inhalation anesthetic. A follow-up on the development of children delivered under these circumstances would, I believe, reveal some interesting data. I had the opportunity of observing one child delivered with what might be called "dianetic hygiene" and can report that there was a greatly accelerated rate of development, including dentition at four months, creeping at five months and quadrupedal walking at six months. It was also noticed that this child had a much more even disposition and was less given to startle reactions and temper manifestations than the average child.

This is, of course, not reported as proof of the value of the hygienic measures suggested; such unusually rapid development might well be purely coincidental. The case is reported merely to suggest a possible method of investigating the trauma of birth to determine the validity of such a concept.

To return to the topic of the possible use of dianetic techniques in the home: it is also a practice in my family to use dianetics to ward off incipient infections. For example, a short time ago, my ten-year-old daughter gave evidence of an upper respiratory infection with rhinorrhea, nasal congestion and a low-grade fever. She was asked to lie down and close her eyes, and it was noticed that she put her hand to her mouth. I asked her, "What does it mean when a person puts his hand to his mouth like you're doing?" She answered, "It might mean that somebody was saying, 'Be quiet.'" I asked her to repeat the phrase, "Be quiet," notice her nasal stuffiness and recall any other association. We were able to develop a scene when she was a tiny baby (I inferred that this occurred immediately after birth), when a man with a mustache was laughing at her and saying, "Be quiet." The obstetrician who delivered her, incidentally, had a mustache; my daughter had not seen him since she was three months old.

At the end of a 20-minute session, during which she yawned copiously, the nasal congestion had disappeared, and there was no more rhinorrhea. She did not develop the cold which would have been the predicted outcome of such a syndrome. She also recalled that her teacher in school that day had found it necessary to tell the class, frequently and emphatically, to be quiet.

Her response also suggests another topic for physiologic research: what are the physiologic effects of yawning? Are there any differences in the oxygen tension of the blood before and after yawning? How does yawning affect the amount of carbon dioxide in the blood? Can therapeutic effects be obtained merely from stimulating a person to yawn? What stimuli will elicit the response of yawning?

Another research project which should be investigated exhaustively is the so-called psychic effect of ACTH and various adrenocorticosteroids. A considerable amount of work is already being done in this field, but it is my impression that the dianetic approach might be more helpful than present better-known methods. One observation which has interested me greatly is the report that patients receiving cortisone will sometimes experience a semi-euphoric state characterized by pleasant insomnia. A similar state has been reported after a successful session in dianetics, wherein the patient lies happily awake for most of the night, recalling events of his past life. Such a parallelism of effect should not be overlooked.

As a matter of opinion—not fact—I suspect that a good many endocrinopathies will respond to the dianetic approach far better than they will to administration of hormones. I have observed one case of exophthalmic goiter in which the exophthalmos decreased almost to the pre-toxic state after psychotherapy of the dianetic type; no other means of treatment was used. Certainly dianetics should not be overlooked as an adjunct to organotherapy.

APPENDIX

In DEVELOPING a patient's recollection of any event, it is necessary to stimulate the recall function by asking questions. Certain perceptual fields are usually investigated, and it has been found that a list of sample questions is of help in covering these fields. Not all these questions need be asked: these are examples of what might be asked.

PERCEPTUAL FIELD	QUESTIONS
1. *Vision*	Is it light or dark? What do you see? How does he or she look? What is he wearing? What is the color of her dress? Does he have a mustache? Does she wear glasses? What is the expression on his face? Is he standing up or sitting down? Where is he standing in relationship to you?

2. *Hearing*   What is being said? Who (or, who do you suppose) is saying that? What are his voice tones? Does he sound angry? Happy? Sad? Fearful? Try to imitate how he sounds. Are there any noises in the background? What do they remind you of?

(Especially useful when recalling birth: What does a new-born baby sound like? Try to imitate the sound.)

3. *Olfaction*   Are there any odors in the room? Are you able to breathe through your nose freely?

4. *Taste*   Any taste in your mouth? How does your mouth feel?

5. *Vestibular*   Is there any sensation of motion? Is there any dizziness associated with this event?

6. *Touch-pressure*   How does your skin feel—dry or moist? Is anything touching you?

7. *Warmth-cold*   Notice the temperature of your surroundings—is it warm or cold?

8. *Proprioception*   What position do you seem to be in? Do your muscles feel tense or relaxed? Try to feel the sensation of your limbs moving.

9. *Deep pressure*   Does your body feel tense? (Generalized pressure, such as experienced in uterine contractions at the beginning of birth, is usually reported as a feeling of tension;

patients seem able to recognize this more easily when it is called "tension," rather than pressure.) Is it constant or intermittent? Regular or irregular?

10. *Pain*

Do you feel any discomfort anywhere? (Use of this euphemism for "pain" seems to enable patients to experience this sensation more easily; a person might avoid "pain" yet will look for "discomfort" without trepidation.) Where do you feel this? Is it constant? What does it remind you of?

11. *Emotion* (*affect*)

How do you feel? What is your mood? If this mood were to get stronger and stronger until you took some action, what action would you take? Would you fight? Run? Cry? Feel like having intercourse? ("Appropriate" activities for anger, fear, grief and love, respectively.) What would you be doing if you weren't laughing? How do you feel—or, what do you think—about a person who would do such a thing?

If patient appears to verbalize his emotions, rather than re-experience them—e.g., if he says, "I feel all right"—ask him: In what part of your body do you feel "all right"? Is there any discomfort which goes along with that feeling?

Notice if patient's verbalizations seem to be at variance with attitudes —e.g., if he says, "I feel ashamed," but has the clenched fists and set jaw suggestive of anger, ask: What makes you think you should be ashamed of this? Who told you that you should be ashamed? Or, try saying to patient in a reproachful tone of voice, "You ought to be ashamed of yourself"; then ask: How does that make you feel?

12. *Associate (parallel) thinking; utilized in obtaining clues as to the patient's characteristic response-pattern.*   What thoughts are going through your mind? Can you think of any parallel situation in recent life? What does this remind you of? Who else acts in this way, or says such things?

——— INDEX ———

225

158486

San Francisco
Medical Center
LIBRARY

University of California
San Francisco
Medical Center
LIBRARY